A New Review of
Pitman Shorthand

Bryan Coombs

A New Review of Pitman Shorthand

NEW ERA EDITION

PITMAN PUBLISHING

First published 1970
Reprinted with minor amendments 1971, 1972
Reprinted 1973

COPYRIGHT

SIR ISAAC PITMAN AND SONS LTD
Pitman House, Parker Street, Kingsway, London WC2B 5PB
P.O. Box 46038, Portal Street, Nairobi, Kenya

SIR ISAAC PITMAN (AUST.) PTY LTD
Pitman House, 158 Bouverie Street, Carlton, Victoria 3053, Australia

PITMAN PUBLISHING COMPANY S.A. LTD
P.O. Box 11231, Johannesburg, South Africa

PITMAN PUBLISHING CORPORATION
6 East 43rd Street, New York, N.Y. 10017, U.S.A.

SIR ISAAC PITMAN (CANADA) LTD
495 Wellington Street West, Toronto 135, Canada

THE COPP CLARK PUBLISHING COMPANY
517 Wellington Street West, Toronto 135, Canada

© Sir Isaac Pitman & Sons Ltd. 1970

ISBN: 0 273 40283 8

The chapter decorations are the work of G. M. Hardie

Text set in 11/12 pt. Monotype Baskerville, printed by letterpress, and bound in Great Britain at The Pitman Press, Bath
G3—(S.650:24)

Preface

Aims of the Book

The aims of *A New Review of Pitman Shorthand* are to review the theory in fifteen easy-to-understand, non-technical chapters; to give a review of short forms (and this includes contractions) and phrases, and to link these signs with the basic theory; to provide ample application material, designed to be meaningful as related to purposeful reading, dictation, and systematic skill building.

Certain rules have been omitted, for example diphones, where it is felt the learning should come through an entirely practical rather than a theoretical approach.

The book is published with a *Key* (S.651) and with accompanying *Sound-Tapes* (S.658).

Application Material

A real effort has been made to give the student theory application exercises not only meaningful as related to the theory content, but also of general interest. There are two long passages in each chapter. One of these sets of passages ranges over a variety of topics of general interest; the other set is designed to give not only practice in shorthand reading and dictation, but also general information as related to office practice. Following the two generalized pieces of material there is a section dealing with correspondence such as is likely to be encountered in a business office. The work in this section concerns one company, and there is continuity running through the book.

Suggested Procedures

It is suggested that the theory sections should be read, and that there should be ample drill on the illustrative words, short forms, and phrases. A concentrated effort must be made to thoroughly automatize each chapter as it is studied. The short forms and phrases have been incorporated into sentence drills. This has been done because experience has shown that these signs are best learned through drilling contextual material.

Preceding each passage there is a preview of difficult outlines. It is suggested that the student should first drill these outlines **very thoroughly.** Each one should be written at least three times, and it is further suggested that as the forms are written the student should repeat the word, or words, *out loud.* In this way the writer sees and hears an outline. Following this drill the passage should be read, preferably out loud, and a note made of any further outlines which it is considered might cause difficulty or hesitation in the subsequent dictation drill. There should now be a further drill of the previewed outlines, plus the outlines selected during the first reading. The passage should then be read through a second time, aiming for a much faster reading.

Many students gain a great deal of benefit from reading and copying printed shorthand material. If this is a procedure that benefits you, then copy the passage, once again saying the words out loud. A class may copy the passage from dictation, sentence by sentence, by individual students.

The student is now ready to take the passage from dictation. If you are working on your own, without teacher assistance, much help will be gained from using a tape recorder for the dictation. Following the dictation there should be at least oral transcription and, whenever possible, there should be some typewritten transcription as well. After checking the note there should be a drilling of any outlines which gave difficulty, and the passage should be dictated again, and it should be possible to increase the rate of speed.

Repeated dictation on the shorter passages, and parts of the longer passages, will be most effective in speed building. Thoroughly previewed and drilled material should form the basis of all speed development.

If these procedures are followed, with amendments and variations as are applicable to individual situations, the student will have a thorough theory review plus a skill building programme that will ultimately lead to confident writing and confident transcription. The material created to give dictation of four, five and six minutes' duration will build up stamina in writing, which is essential to the student preparing for examinations and for long bouts of dictation in the office.

The correspondence section can be dealt with in exactly the same way. It is suggested that this section is particularly meaningful in building typewriting transcription techniques to a high level of competency. The aim should be the production of mailable transcripts.

For the student working alone the longhand key to this book is essential. It is strongly urged that all students work with the longhand key. Valuable classroom time can be saved by reading and preparing exercises at home. Students using the key will be able to work at their own rate. Teachers using this approach will have more time to give individual guidance where it is needed.

Learning Load
The book has been designed to level out the learning load. However, since it was also part of the concept of the book to relate the short forms and phrases to the particular theory section encompassing them, there are one or two chapters which are rather "heavy" in short form and phrase review. This should not cause the student much difficulty, since the book is in the nature of a review rather than a basic learning medium. Chapter 5 (The R Hook) has a high short form content, and

such a chapter should be studied at a slower pace. In the first two chapters some short forms are reviewed which are not related to the theory of those chapters.

Order of Learning
It is possible to study any one chapter as a separate and complete unit of learning. It is suggested, however, that the student would gain much benefit from studying the first six chapters in their order of presentation. It is considered that these six sections of theory cause the most difficulty.

Intersections
Intersections are reviewed at the beginning of the book and are incorporated into the application material throughout. In this way the student will acquire a working knowledge of these most functional devices, and be encouraged to use them all the time.

Appreciation
I would like to thank the publishers for their invitation to me to write this book and for their co-operation throughout its preparation. My special thanks go to Marion Angus, who has been a source of inspiration to me over many years of shorthand writing, for the many hours she devoted to editing the theory sections. She gave unstintingly of her off duty time during visits I have made to New York in recent years.

Bryan Coombs   *Chartered Shorthand Reporter*
Senior Lecturer in Secretarial Studies
Newcastle upon Tyne Polytechnic

Contents

1 Prefixes

1 (a) *CON(N)*- or *COM(M)*- is represented by a dot written at the beginning of the following stroke. The position of the outline is decided by the first vowel after the prefix:

conduct   consist   commit   communication

(b) In the middle of a word *CON*-, *COM*-, *CUM*-, or *COG*- is represented by disjoining:

reconsider   disconnect   recommend   recognize   circumference

2 *ACCOM*- or *ACCOMMO*- is represented by *K* joined or disjoined. The outline is written in the first position:

accommodation   accomplish   accommodate

1

3 *MAGNA-*, *MAGNE-*, or *MAGNI-* is represented by *M* disjoined. The outline is written in the first position:

magnitude   magnificent   magnanimous

4 *INTRO-* is represented by a joined double length *N*. The outline is written in the third position:

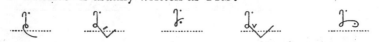

introduce   introductory   introspect

5 *TRANS-* is usually written as *TRS*:

transfer   transport   translate   transpire   transmission

In some words it is easier or more legible to write *TRNS-* as in

transaction

6 *SELF-* is represented by a disjoined *S* Circle written in the second place vowel position. The outlines are written in the second position:

self-defence   self-made   self-supporting

7 *SELF-CON-* is represented by the *S* Circle written in place of the *CON-* dot. The outlines are written in the second position:

self-control   self-confident   self-contained

8 *IN-* before *ST-R*, *SK-R* and upward *H*, is represented by a small hook. The outlines are written in the third position:

instruct   instrument   inhabit   inherit

Note: When the prefix *IN-* means *NOT*, the stroke *N* is always used:

inhospitable   inscrutable   inhuman

9 *IL-*, *IR-* are represented by downward *L* or *R* in negative words when the basic rule permits:

irresolute *but* resolute   irrelevant *but* relevant

10 *IM-*, *IN-*, or *UN-* is represented in negative words by repeating the *M* or *N*:

immortal   innocuous   unnecessary

CHECK

Fill your pen and/or sharpen your pencils each day

SHORT FORMS

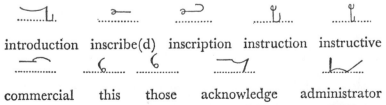

introduction   inscribe(d)   inscription   instruction   instructive

commercial   this   those   acknowledge   administrator

altogether anything architect-ure-al bankruptcy capable

certificate contingency manufacture(d) manufacturer

peculiar-ity together yesterday

SHORT FORM DRILL

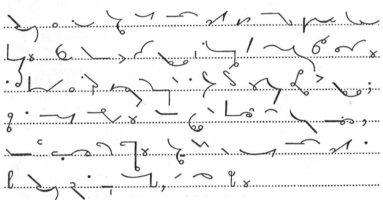

INTERSECTIONS

Stroke	Word Represented	As in	
	party	political party	
	bank	local bank	
	bill	enclosed bill	
	attention	call attention	
	department	Foreign Department	

...../.....	charge	excess charge	
...../.....	journal	commercial journal	
...—....	company	your company	
...—....	capital	capital expenditure	
...—....	government	local government	
		British Government	
...—....	beginning	at the beginning	
		from the beginning	
...\....	form	several forms	
...(....	month	this month	
...(....	authority	director's authority	
...~....	national	national interests	

INTERSECTION DRILL

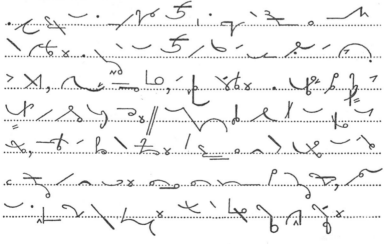

PREVIEW

interview		punctually	
organization		magnificent	
considerable		accomplish	
complete		self-confident	
transport		contingencies	
contact		originals	
embarrassment		transcribe	
instructions		transcription	
questions		inconsistencies	
prospects		awkward	
shirt		counsellors	
irresistible		precisely	
fancy		committing	

Interviews

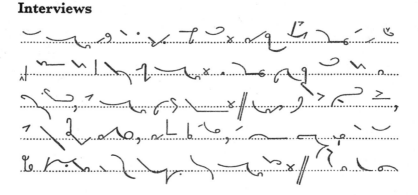

6

PREVIEW

fascinating		Manhattan ✕	
describe		accomplish	
defensive		delightful	
accommodation		transplanted	
inhabitants		discerning	
humid		Greenwich ✕	
atmosphere		compelled	

inhospitable		entertainments	
inconsiderate		Rockettes X	
swelter		orchestra	
reputation		precision	
courtesy		extravaganza X	
favourite		recommend	
thoroughfare			

New York

9

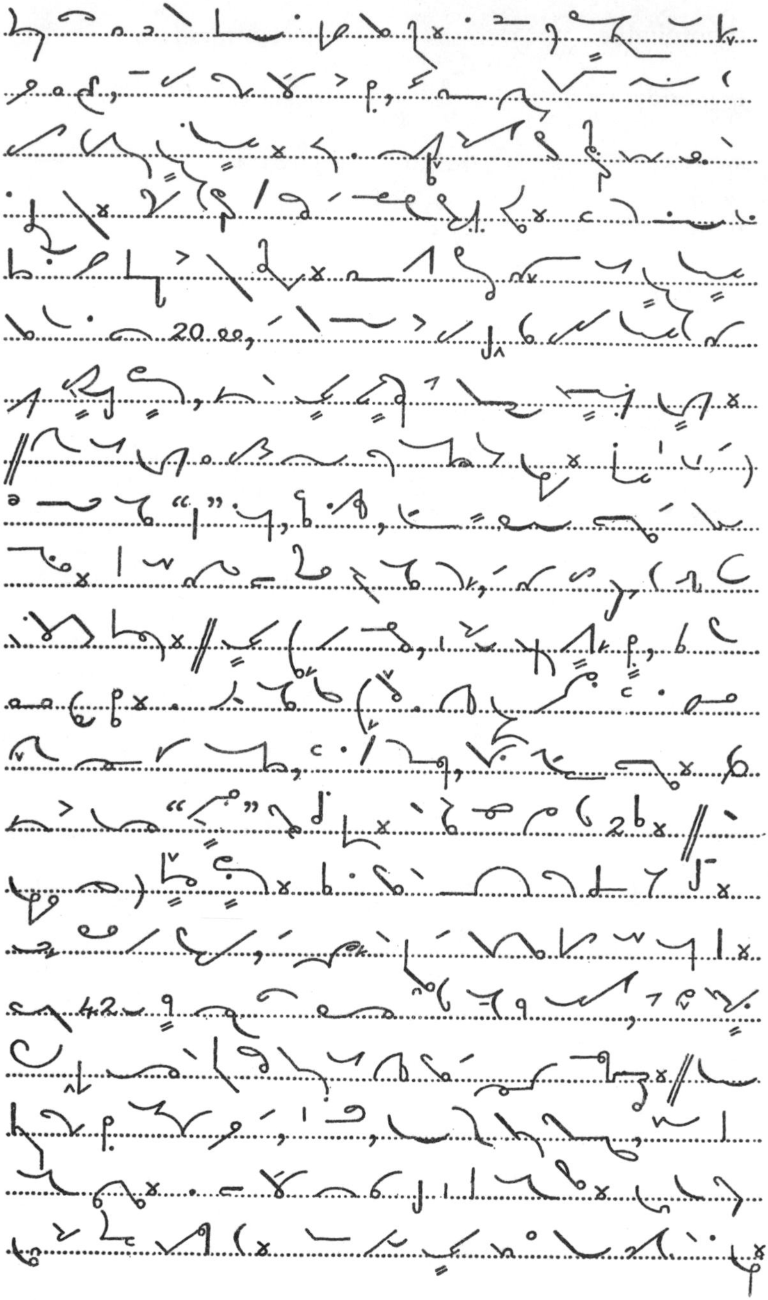

CORRESPONDENCE

All correspondence is to or from:

    International Importers and Exporters Limited
    Commerce House
    Regent Street
    London W1

Letter to:

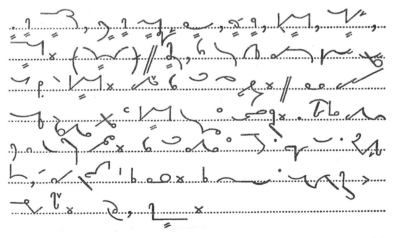

Letter to:

2 Suffixes

1 -*ING* is represented by the stroke *NG*, and the light dot -*ING*.

The light dot -*ING* is used where a stroke *NG* would be inconvenient as for example:

(a)

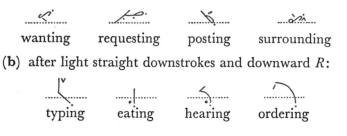

wanting   requesting   posting   surrounding

(b) after light straight downstrokes and downward *R*:

typing   eating   hearing   ordering

Note: When dot -*ING* is used for the singular, a dash is used for the plural:

surroundings   postings   mornings   meetings

(c) usually after short forms:

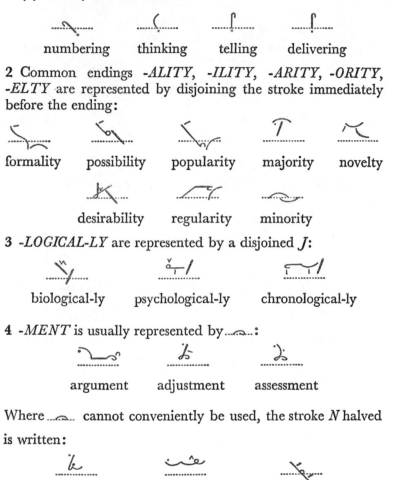

numbering   thinking   telling   delivering

2 Common endings *-ALITY, -ILITY, -ARITY, -ORITY, -ELTY* are represented by disjoining the stroke immediately before the ending:

formality   possibility   popularity   majority   novelty

desirability   regularity   minority

3 *-LOGICAL-LY* are represented by a disjoined *J*:

biological-ly   psychological-ly   chronological-ly

4 *-MENT* is usually represented by ⌢ :

argument   adjustment   assessment

Where ⌢ cannot conveniently be used, the stroke *N* halved is written:

achievement   announcement   postponement

5 *-MENTAL, -MENTALLY, -MENTALITY* are represented by ⌢ disjoined:

fundamental-ly   experimental-ly   instrumental-ly

13

6 -*SHIP* is represented by joined or disjoined:

friendship   leadership   citizenship   membership

7 -*FULNESS*, -*LESSNESS*, -*LOUSNESS* are represented by

 and disjoined:

cheerfulness   thoughtfulness   forgetfulness   carelessness

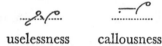

uselessness   callousness

8 (*a*) -*WARD*, -*WART* are represented by a half-length *W*:

backward   reward   forward   stalwart   thwart

(*b*) -*YARD* is represented by a half-length *Y*:

backyard   shipyard

CHECK

**Posture—feet on the floor, weight of
the body on the non-writing arm**

SHORT FORMS

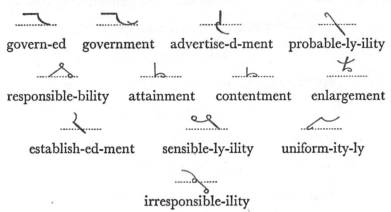

govern-ed   government   advertise-d-ment   probable-ly-ility

responsible-bility   attainment   contentment   enlargement

establish-ed-ment   sensible-ly-ility   uniform-ity-ly

irresponsible-ility

SHORT FORM DRILL

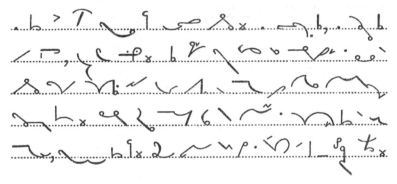

INTERSECTIONS

Stroke	*Word Represented*	*As in*	
	valuation	today's valuation	
	morning	this morning	
	mark	trade mark	
	liberal	liberal discount	

15

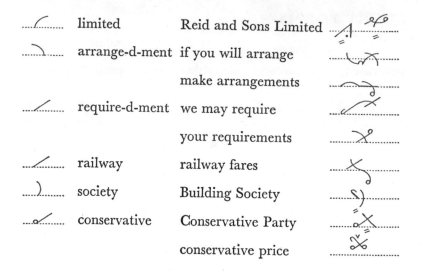

...(...	limited	Reid and Sons Limited
...) ...	arrange-d-ment	if you will arrange
		make arrangements
...∕ ...	require-d-ment	we may require
		your requirements
...∕ ...	railway	railway fares
...) ...	society	Building Society
...α∕ ...	conservative	Conservative Party
		conservative price

INTERSECTION DRILL

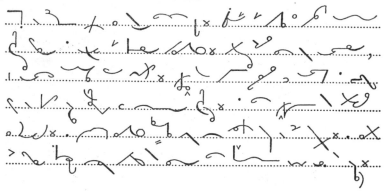

OMISSION OF CONSONANTS

P, K, G and T when lightly sounded may be omitted:

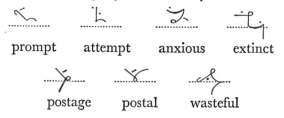

prompt   attempt   anxious   extinct

postage   postal   wasteful

PREVIEW

technological		preferably	
fundamental		seaside	
postponement		desirability	
rewards		backyard	
uselessness		screens	
tremendously		novelty	
experimental		minority	
athletics		announcements	
instrumental		forward	
consumer		national	
chronological		friendship	
activities		individual	

Time for Leisure

[shorthand outlines]

17

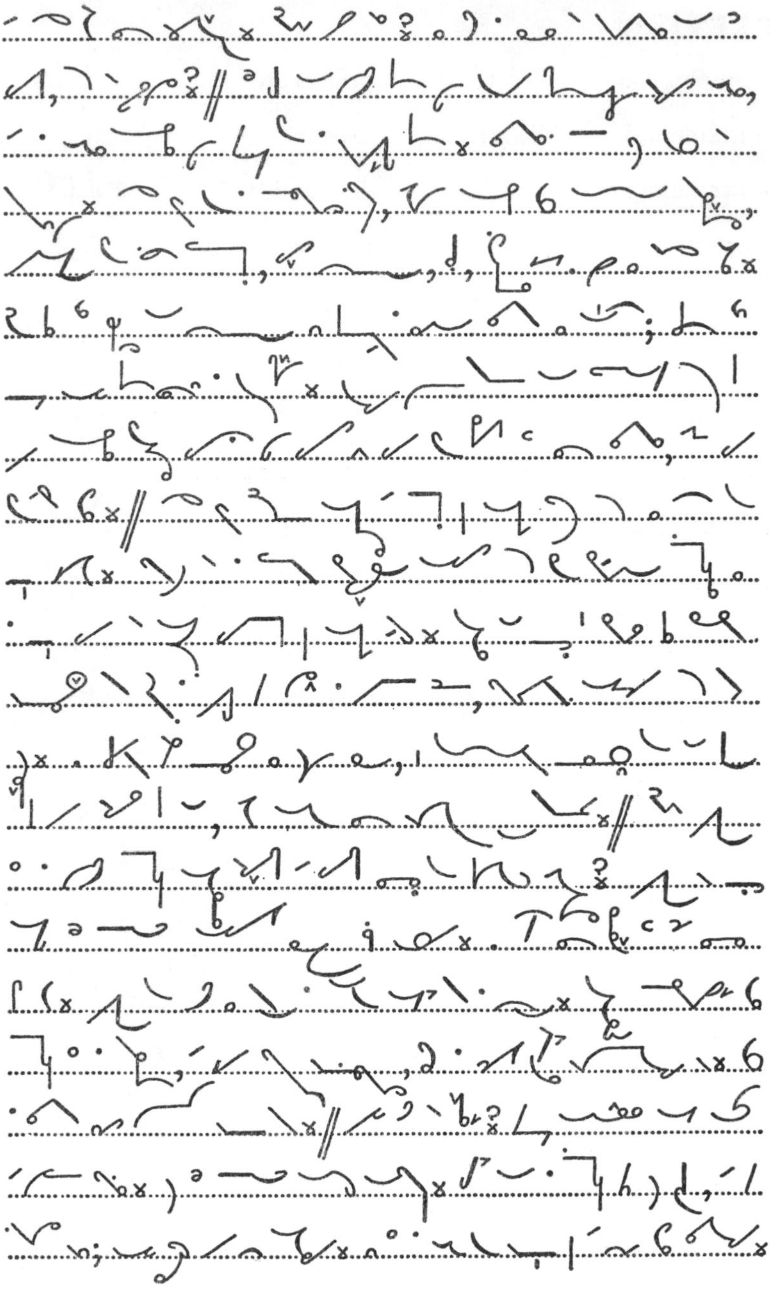

PREVIEW

secretary	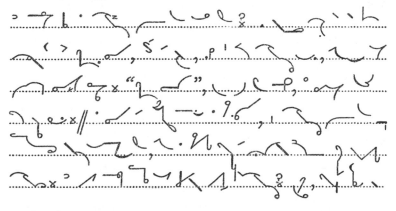	leadership	
beautiful		appointment	
vanished		supervisory	
command		tolerated	
qualifications		outings	
productivity		psychological	
qualities		assessment	
welcomed		competitive	
assistance		formality	
thoughtfulness		instructions	
majority		dynamic	
punctuality		achievement	

Secretarial Qualities

19

20

CORRESPONDENCE
Letter from:

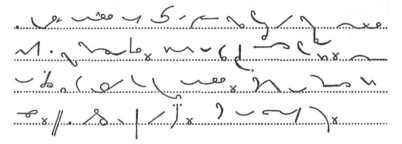

Memo from the Director to Sales Manager, today's date:

3 Hook L

1 A small hook to straight strokes on the same side as the Circle *S* adds *L*:

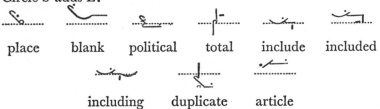

place   blank   political   total   include   included

including   duplicate   article

2 (a) The sound of *S* as the consonant coming immediately before *L* Hook is written inside the hook:

supply   cycle   splendid   supplement   settle

(b) When occurring medially both circle and hook are shown:

display   physical   exclusive   possibly

22

3 A large initial hook on the inside of curves adds *L*:

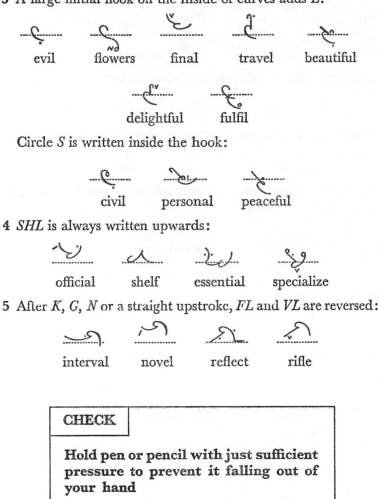

evil   flowers   final   travel   beautiful

delightful   fulfil

Circle *S* is written inside the hook:

civil   personal   peaceful

4 *SHL* is always written upwards:

official   shelf   essential   specialize

5 After *K, G, N* or a straight upstroke, *FL* and *VL* are reversed:

interval   novel   reflect   rifle

CHECK

Hold pen or pencil with just sufficient pressure to prevent it falling out of your hand

---

SHORT FORMS

people   belief(ve)(d)   tell   till   deliver(ed)(y)

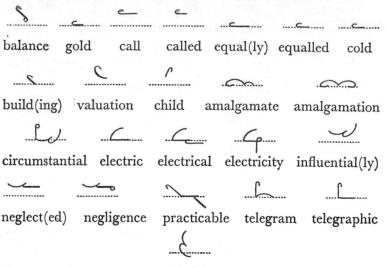

balance gold call called equal(ly) equalled cold

build(ing) valuation child amalgamate amalgamation

circumstantial electric electrical electricity influential(ly)

neglect(ed) negligence practicable telegram telegraphic

thankful

PHRASING

at all   by all   I believe   able to

SHORT FORM AND PHRASING DRILL

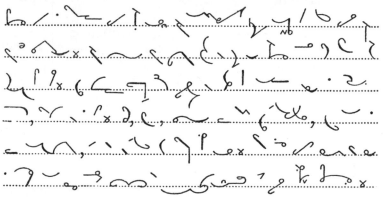

PREVIEW

throughout		customarily	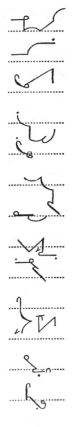
telephonist		colleague	
tactful		overheard	
delicate		confidential	
potential		conversations	
delightful		inevitable	
switchboard		signal	
specifically		periodically	
demonstration		acceptable	
expressions		trivial	
pronunciation		tolerated	
abandoned		speculate	
available		deliberations	

Telephone Technique

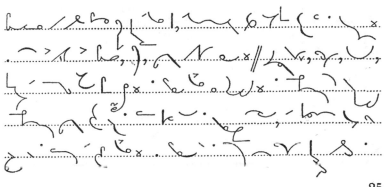

25

PREVIEW

commonplace		cholera	
privileged		documentary	
radical		injections	
aeroplane		vaccinations	
circulation		diseases	
formalities		financial	
exceptions		comparatively	
passport		negotiable	
neighbouring		professional	

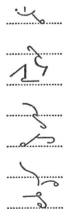

27

reciprocal 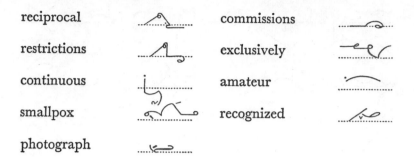 commissions

restrictions exclusively

continuous amateur

smallpox recognized

photograph

Travel

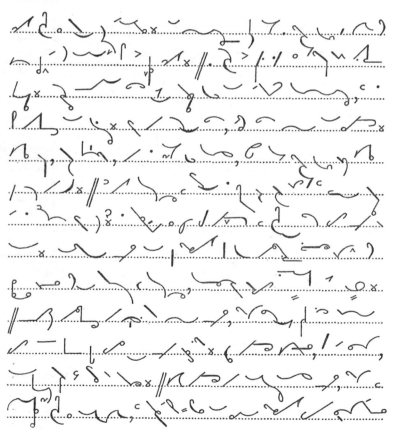

28

CORRESPONDENCE
A letter to:

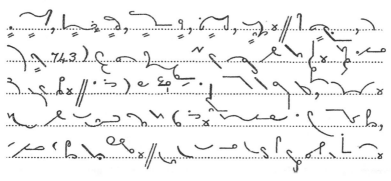

A letter from:

4 Shun Hook

The sound of *SHUN*, however it is spelled, is represented by a large final hook.

It is written:

1 Inside curves:

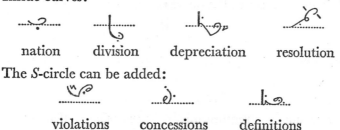

nation   division   depreciation   resolution

The *S*-circle can be added:

violations   concessions   definitions

2 When attached to straight strokes *SHUN*-hook is written:

(**a**) on the opposite side to an initial hook or circle, to keep the straight stroke straight:

consideration   creations   section   stations

(b) on the opposite side to the last vowel if there is no hook or circle, to assist in vowel indication:

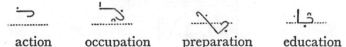

action   occupation   preparation   education

(c) on the right side of simple *T, D* or *J*, to keep the writing line moving:

condition   quotation   magician   additions

3 After 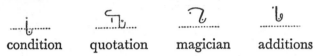 and 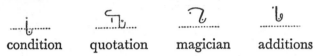 the *SHUN*-hook is written away from the curve, in order to keep the straight stroke straight:

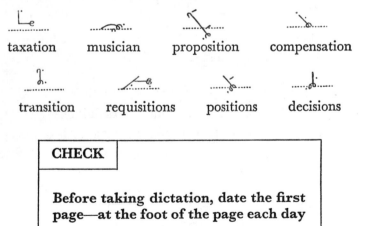

affection   notification   location   selection

vocation

4 After *S* or *NS* circle the sound of *SHUN* is represented by a hook which is a continuation of the circle:

taxation   musician   proposition   compensation

transition   requisitions   positions   decisions

CHECK

Before taking dictation, date the first page—at the foot of the page each day

---

SHORT FORMS

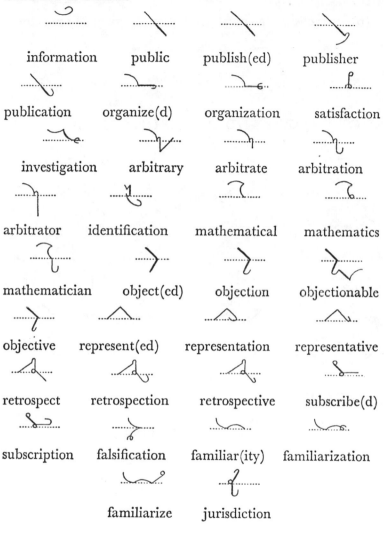

information   public   publish(ed)   publisher

publication   organize(d)   organization   satisfaction

investigation   arbitrary   arbitrate   arbitration

arbitrator   identification   mathematical   mathematics

mathematician   object(ed)   objection   objectionable

objective   represent(ed)   representation   representative

retrospect   retrospection   retrospective   subscribe(d)

subscription   falsification   familiar(ity)   familiarization

familiarize   jurisdiction

PHRASING

(a) *ocean:*   Atlantic Ocean   Pacific Ocean

33

(b) *association:* political association   medical association

your association

SHORT FORM AND PHRASING DRILL

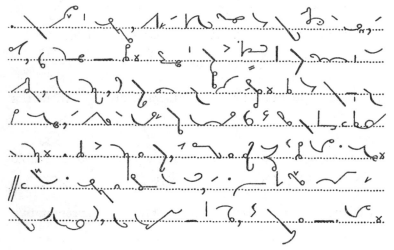

PREVIEW

impression		objectionable	
apprehensive		theoretical	
apprehension		instructions	
personnel		hesitation	
induction		clarification	
departmental		co-operation	
qualifications		tension	

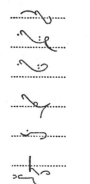
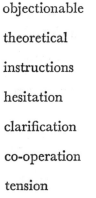
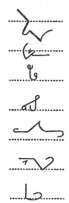

34

justification	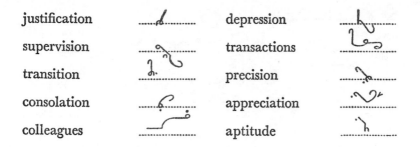	depression	
supervision		transactions	
transition		precision	
consolation		appreciation	
colleagues		aptitude	

First Impressions

35

PREVIEW

vocabulary		interpretation	
administrations		discretion	
initiation		interruptions	
terminology		comprehension	
intention		communication	
seconder		comprehend	
conclusion		transcription	
resolution		protection	
constitution		participation	
illustration		mover	

quorum

frequently

secretary

A Question of Comprehension

37

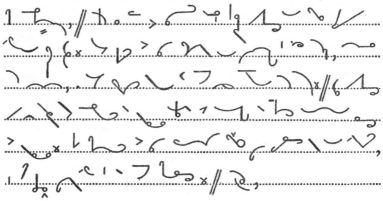

CORRESPONDENCE
Prepare a circular letter to go to all customers, today's date.

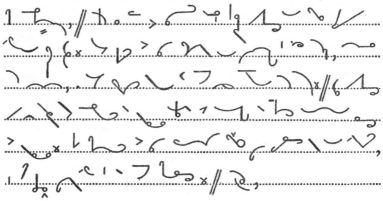

Memo to all staff from the Manager:

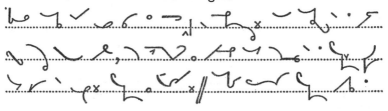

5 R Hook

1 A small hook to straight strokes on the opposite side to the Circle *S* adds *R*:

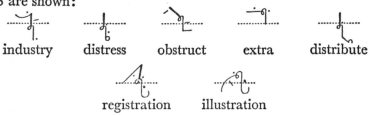

price   propose   directors   increase   degree   teacher

2 (a) When *S*, *ST* or *SWAY* occur immediately before the sound of consonant + *R* they are written on the same side as the Hook *R*:

spring   strange   separate   steeper   sweater   sweeter

(b) In the middle of an outline both the hook and the Circle *S* are shown:

industry   distress   obstruct   extra   distribute

registration   illustration

3 (a) A small hook on the inside of curves adds *R*:

former   rumour   afraid

(b) Circle *S* is written inside the hook:

safer   dishonour   sooner   suffer

4 *S HR* and *ZHR* are always written downwards:

pressure   shrug   shrill   shrewd   enclosure

5 *FR, VR, THR* and *ThR* are reversed:
(a) when standing alone and with no initial vowel:

freight   fry   three   freeze

(b) to obtain an easier joining:

river   Africa   discover   anniversary

6 There are two uses of the *R* hook and *L* hook series.
(a) They are used as consonants:

across   blue   shrub   throw   fluid

(b) They are used as syllables and when necessary the vowel
between hook and consonant is shown:

engineer   atmosphere   parcel   culminate   political   course

SHORT FORMS

nor (in our)　　near　　owner　　more　　remark(ed)

Mr　　mere　　sure　　pleasure　　over　　however

Dr　　dear　　during　　truth　　principle　　principal(ly)

liberty　　member　　remember(ed)　　number(ed)　　chair

cheer　　care　　according　　from　　great　　guard

larger　　opportunity　　spirit　　surprise　　their　　there

toward　　towards　　tried　　trade　　very　　character

characteristic　　cross-examine(d)(ation)　　mortgage

jurisdiction　　parliamentary　　practice　　practise(d)　　prejudice

preliminary　　probable　　production　　productive　　proficient(cy)

project(ed)　　proportion(ed)　　proportionate(ly)　　prospect

42

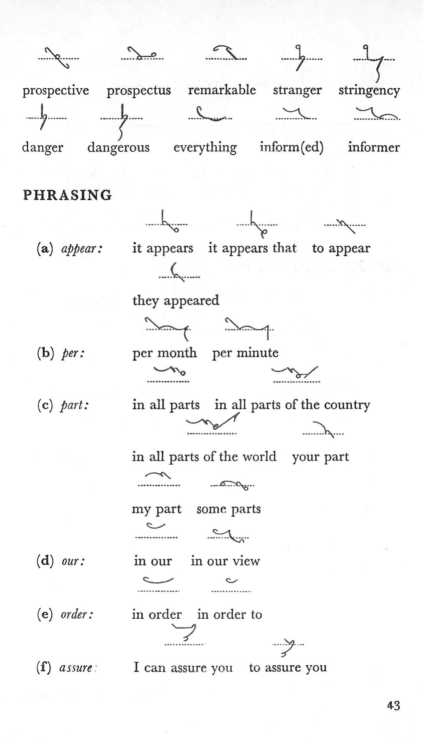

prospective   prospectus   remarkable   stranger   stringency

danger   dangerous   everything   inform(ed)   informer

PHRASING

(a) *appear:*   it appears   it appears that   to appear

they appeared

(b) *per:*   per month   per minute

(c) *part:*   in all parts   in all parts of the country

in all parts of the world   your part

my part   some parts

(d) *our:*   in our   in our view

(e) *order:*   in order   in order to

(f) *assure:*   I can assure you   to assure you

43

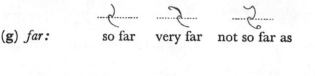

(g) *far:*   so far   very far   not so far as

> **CHECK**
>
> Leave a side margin—use it for queries, corrections and helpful notes

---

SHORT FORM DRILL

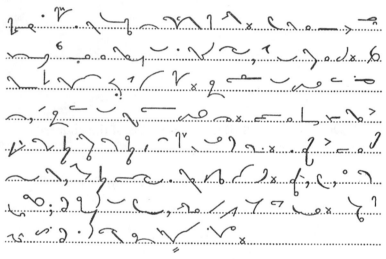

PHRASING DRILL

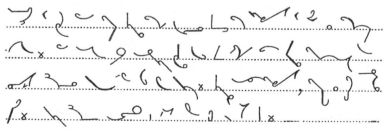

PREVIEW

appreciate		theory	
incredibly		reverse	
difficulties		bothers	
identification		impeding	
proficiency		distressing	
system		shoulders	
accurate		comprehension	
vocabulary		strictly	
productive		occur	
stranger		frequently	
hesitation		free	
ultimate		offer	

Progress in Shorthand

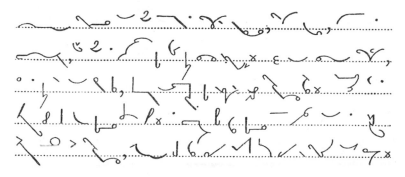

45

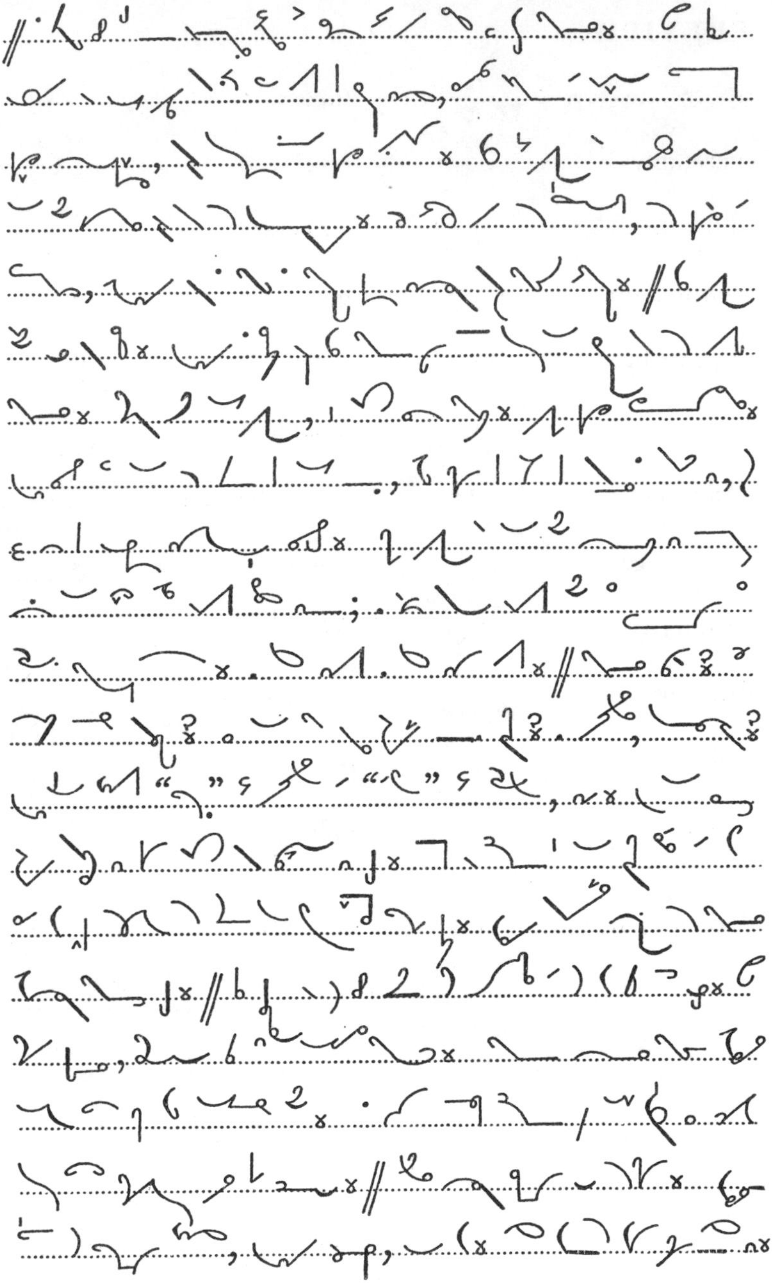

PREVIEW

tourist		description	
attraction		Circus	
travellers		traffic	
pilgrimage		comfortable	
British		visitors	
ancestry		accommodation	
corners		thrifty	
parents		elsewhere	
forbears		democratic	
theatre		centuries	
exhibitions		decorated	
gatherings		specialist	

London

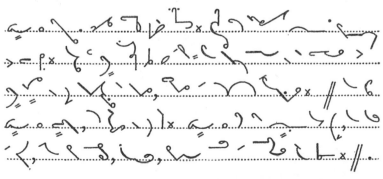

47

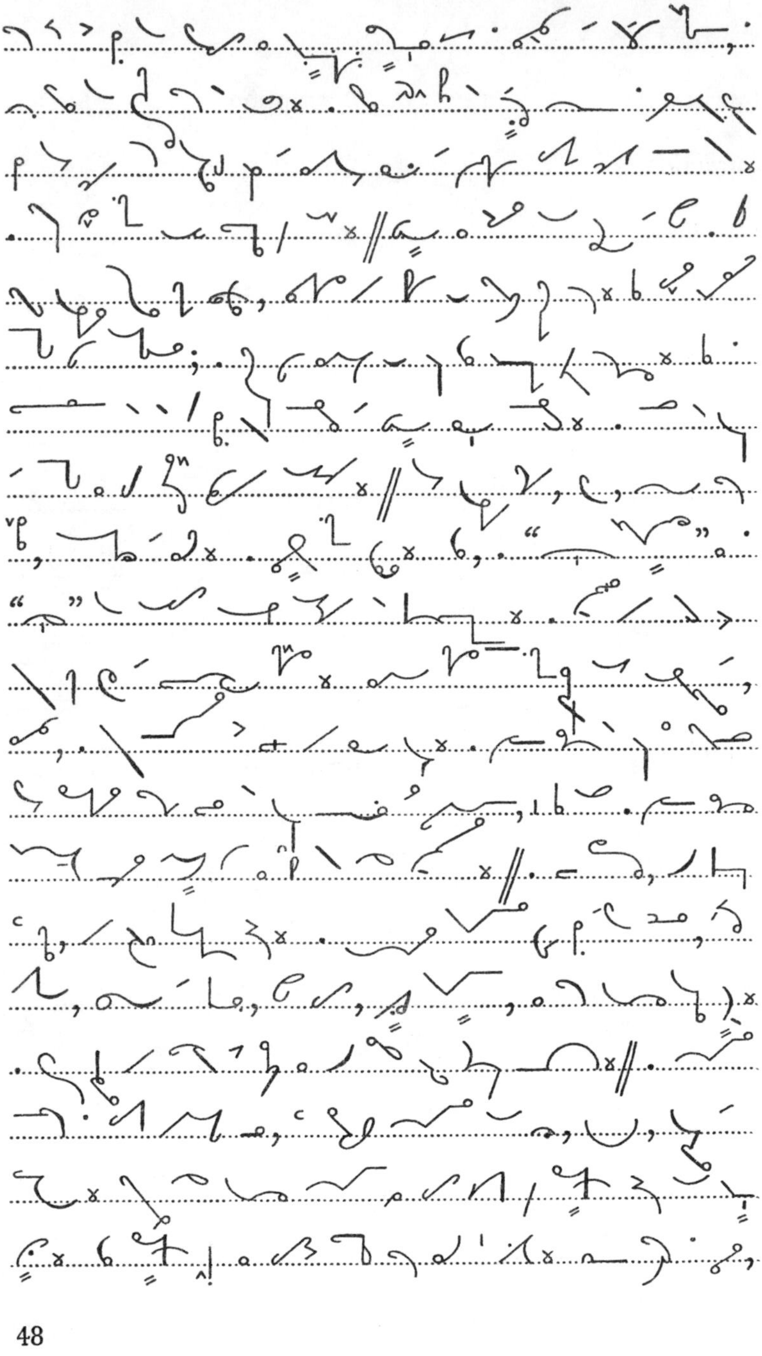

[Shorthand text]

CORRESPONDENCE

Letter to:

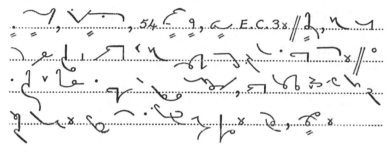

Expand and display the following information for an advertisement in the daily press:

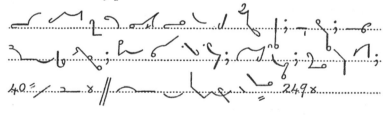

6 The Consonant R

There are two forms for *R*, the downward *AR* ⌒, and the upward *RAY* ╱.

RAY (Upward *R*) is used:
1 Usually, when *R* begins a word:

| road | return | response | relation |

2 Usually in the middle of an outline:

| park | authority | carrying |

3 When a vowel follows *R* at the end of a word:

| history | story | borrow | carry |

4 After *FS, VS, NS, KS* and *GS*:

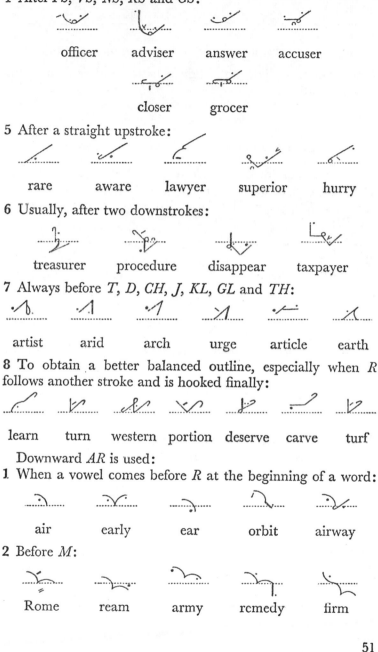

officer   adviser   answer   accuser

closer   grocer

5 After a straight upstroke:

rare   aware   lawyer   superior   hurry

6 Usually, after two downstrokes:

treasurer   procedure   disappear   taxpayer

7 Always before *T, D, CH, J, KL, GL* and *TH*:

artist   arid   arch   urge   article   earth

8 To obtain a better balanced outline, especially when *R* follows another stroke and is hooked finally:

learn   turn   western   portion   deserve   carve   turf

Downward *AR* is used:

1. When a vowel comes before *R* at the beginning of a word:

air   early   ear   orbit   airway

2 Before *M*:

Rome   ream   army   remedy   firm

3 Usually when *R* ends the word:

appear   error   assure   colour   repair

4 Sometimes medially to obtain a better outline or a distinguishing outline:

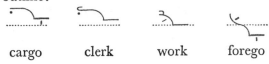

cargo   clerk   work   forego

Other uses of downward *AR* are:

1 At the end of an outline *AR* is halved and thickened to represent *RD*, provided no sounded vowel comes between *R* and *D*:

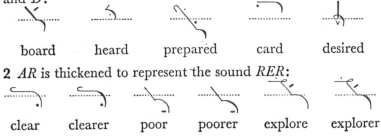

board   heard   prepared   card   desired

2 *AR* is thickened to represent the sound *RER*:

clear   clearer   poor   poorer   explore   explorer

CHECK
More than double any double-length strokes. Less than halve any half-length strokes

SHORT FORMS

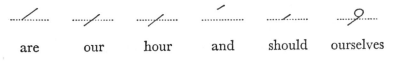

are   our   hour   and   should   ourselves

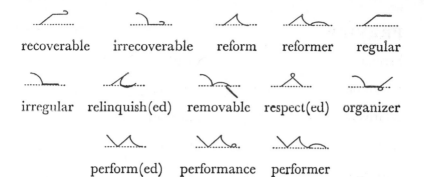

recoverable   irrecoverable   reform   reformer   regular

irregular   relinquish(ed)   removable   respect(ed)   organizer

perform(ed)   performance   performer

PHRASING

In certain words either the upward or downward form of *R* may be used in phrasing:

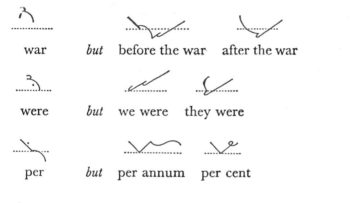

war   *but*   before the war   after the war

were   *but*   we were   they were

per   *but*   per annum   per cent

SHORT FORM AND PHRASING DRILL

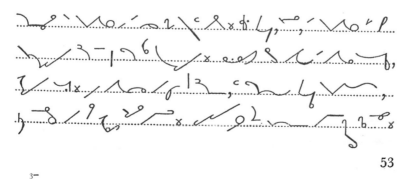

PREVIEW

arrival	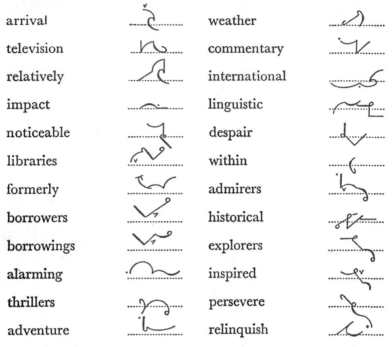	weather	
television		commentary	
relatively		international	
impact		linguistic	
noticeable		despair	
libraries		within	
formerly		admirers	
borrowers		historical	
borrowings		explorers	
alarming		inspired	
thrillers		persevere	
adventure		relinquish	

Reading

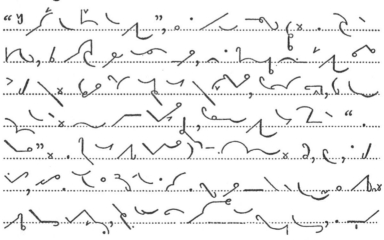

54

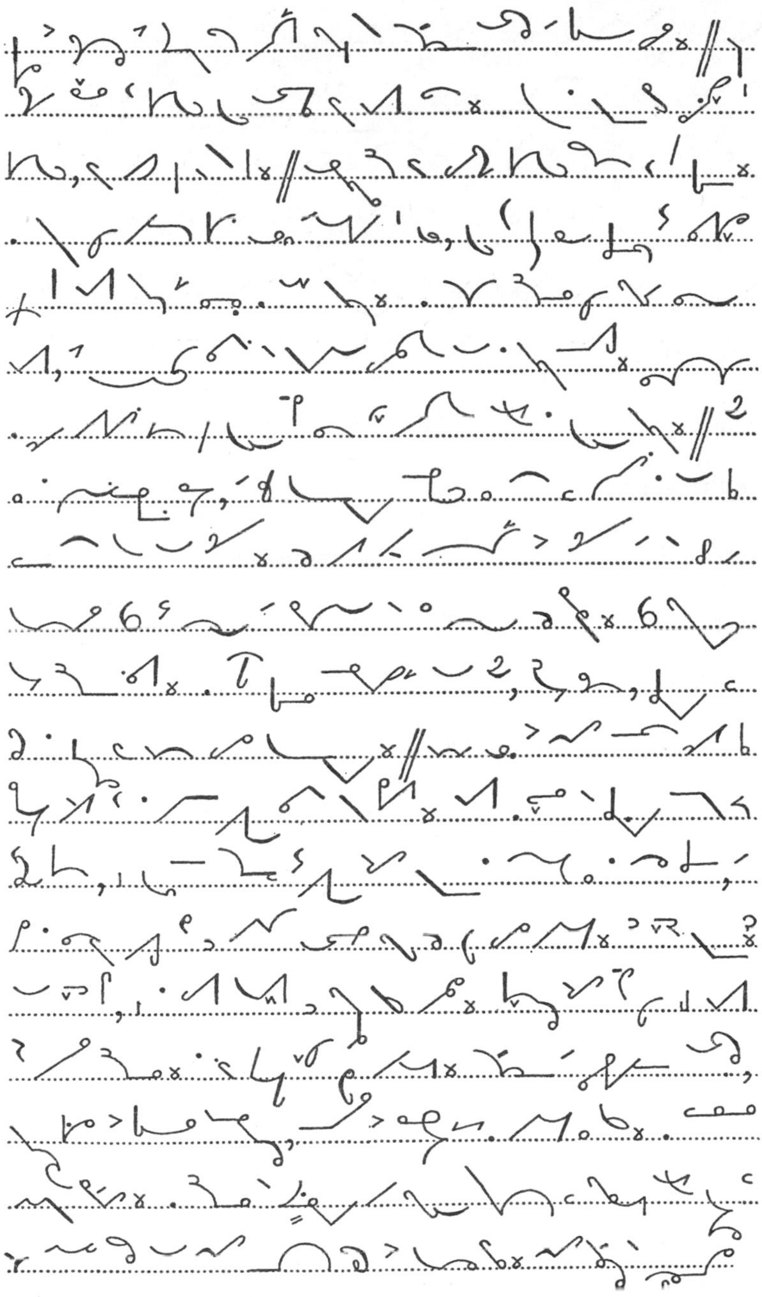

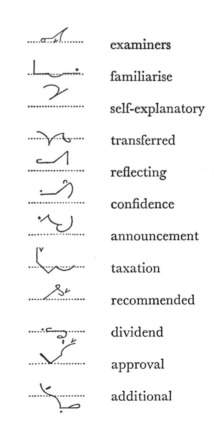

PREVIEW

secretarial		examiners	
technique		familiarise	
machinery		self-explanatory	
irrelevant		transferred	
clarity		reflecting	
accuracy		confidence	
artificial		announcement	
typewritten		taxation	
recipient		recommended	
conclusions		dividend	
burial		approval	
forecast		additional	

56

Reports

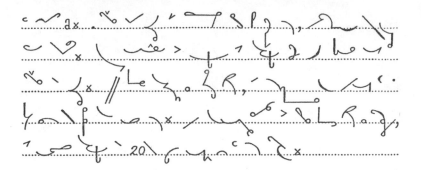

CORRESPONDENCE

You are secretary to the Sales Manager, Robert Richardson, who is away on a business trip to Kenya and Uganda, East Africa, arriving in Nairobi today. Before meeting any business associates he is taking a three-day holiday in the game reserve near Nairobi.

The following are notes of a telephone message you have just received from an important supplier in Kampala, Uganda, who Mr Richardson was going to visit on the fourth day of his official functions:

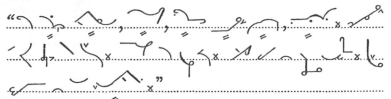

Send a telegram to Mr Richardson, New Stanley Hotel, Nairobi, advising him of the situation.

Memo from the Manager to the Supervisor, Secretarial Services Bureau, today's date, subject *Interviews*.

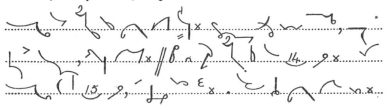

7 W and Related Consonants

The stroke *WAY* is generally used to represent the sound of *W*:

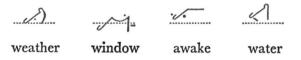

    weather   **window**   awake   water

1 *W* at the beginning of a word and followed by *K, G, M,* or upward or downward *R* is represented by a small semi-circle:

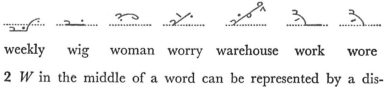

weekly   wig   woman   worry   warehouse   work   wore

2 *W* in the middle of a word can be represented by a disjoined semi-circle, if *WAY* is inconvenient or too lengthy:

    (**a**) *W* followed by a dot vowel is represented by a left semi-circle in the position of the vowel following the *W* sound:

frequently   goodwill   subsequent

(b) *W* followed by a dash vowel is represented by a right semi-circle in the position of the vowel following the *W* sound:

quality   qualify   somewhat

Note. In practice many outlines can be read without the semi-circle, in which case it may be omitted.

3 *WH* is represented by the stroke ⌐⟋ :

wheat   where   wherever   white

4 *WL* is represented by the stroke ⌐ :

will   wealth   welfare   welcomed

5 *WHL* is represented by the stroke ⌐ :

wheel   whale   while   meanwhile

6 *W* combined with the sound of *Kay* or *Gay* is represented by ⌐ ⌐ , giving the sound of *KWAY* and *GWAY*:

quick   require   quantity   acquaintance

delinquent   linguist   squander   square

60

SHORT FORMS

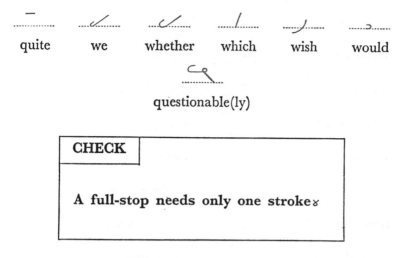

quite	we	whether	which	wish	would

questionable(ly)

CHECK

A full-stop needs only one stroke⌄

PHRASING
The sound of *W* may be omitted in phrases:

this week	next week	you will	very well

you were

Note. We will ⌒, **in which the *W* is retained.**

SHORT FORM AND PHRASING DRILL

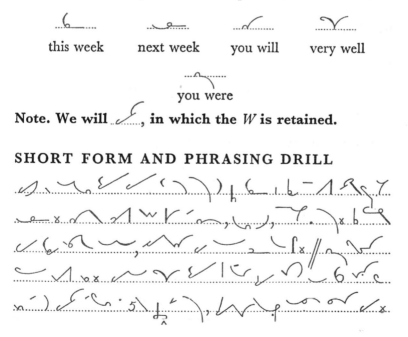

PREVIEW

working		worst	
awareness		farewell	
questionable		acquaintances	
consequences		acquiring	
permanently		outings	
continuity		achievement	
someone		independence	
honestly		remunerations	
meanwhile		splash	
irreplaceable		squander	
sensible		disaster	
liquids		worthwhile	

Welcome to the Working Ranks

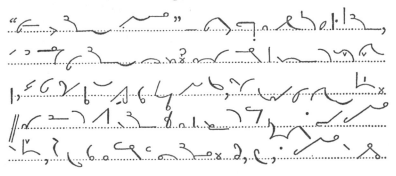

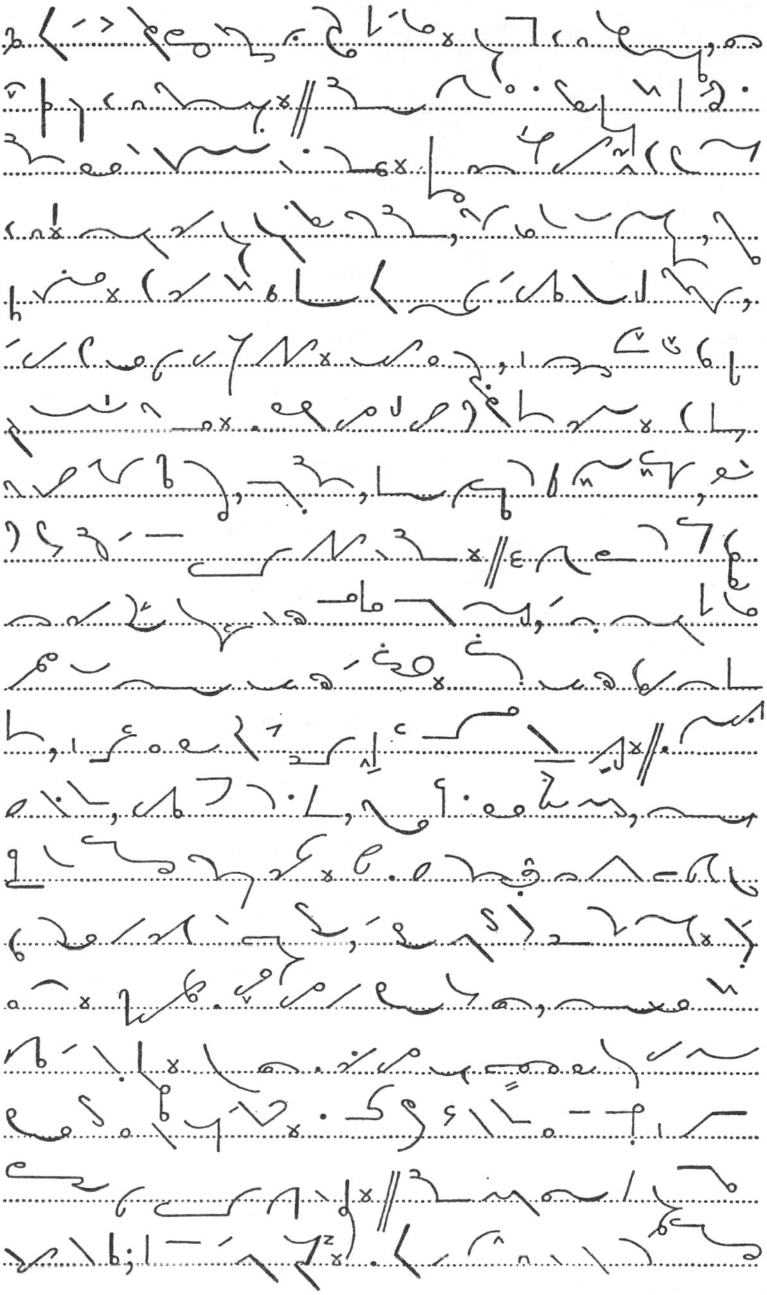

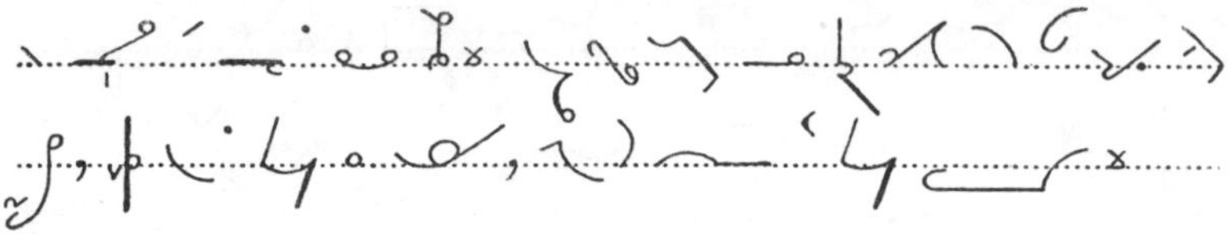

PREVIEW

comparatively		participate	
ocean		warmer	
nowadays		emigrating	
stewardesses		liners	
attendants		competition	
workers		departure	
banquets		quantities	
newcomer		persuaded	
passengers		gymnasium	
harbour		wanderlust	
schedules		available	
social		homeward	

All at Sea

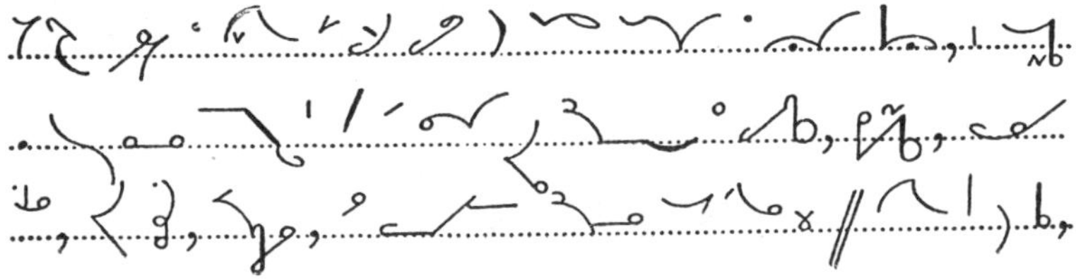

CORRESPONDENCE

Mr Richardson has telephoned you from Nairobi. The following are your notes of that conversation:

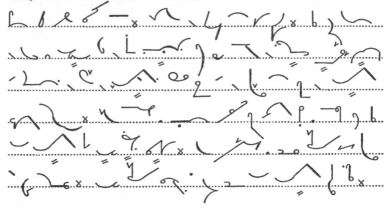

Send telegram to Raymond Roberts, Manager, African Curios Limited, Kampala, Uganda. Memo to all departments advising them of changes in Mr Richardson's itinerary.

Letter to:

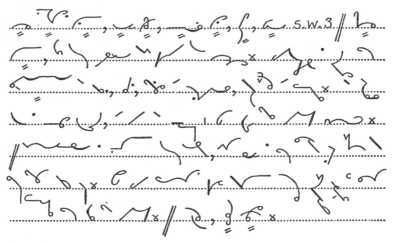

8 Consonant L

Stroke *L* is generally written upward:

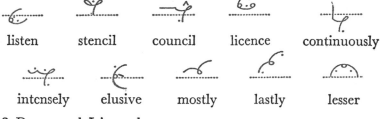

load   land   letter   dealer   coal   detail   envelope

1 When *L* immediately precedes a circle and curve or follows a curve and circle it is written in the same direction as the circle:

listen   stencil   council   licence   continuously

intensely   elusive   mostly   lastly   lesser

2 Downward *L* is used:

   (**a**) usually after *N* and *ING*:

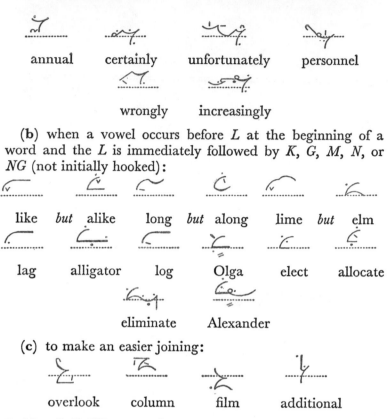

annual   certainly   unfortunately   personnel

wrongly   increasingly

(b) when a vowel occurs before *L* at the beginning of a word and the *L* is immediately followed by *K, G, M, N,* or *NG* (not initially hooked):

like   *but*   alike   long   *but*   along   lime   *but*   elm

lag   alligator   log   Olga   elect   allocate

eliminate   Alexander

(c) to make an easier joining:

overlook   column   film   additional

3 After *F, V, SK* or a straight upstroke, *L* is written downward if no vowel follows and upward if a vowel follows:

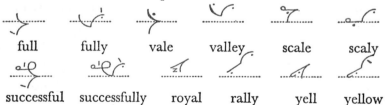

full   fully   vale   valley   scale   scaly

successful   successfully   royal   rally   yell   yellow

4 When downward *L* can be written it may be thickened to add the sound of *R*:

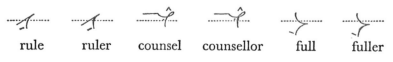

rule   ruler   counsel   counsellor   full   fuller

68

5 Downward *L* may be halved and thickened to add the sound of *D* provided that there is no sounded vowel between the *L* and *D*:

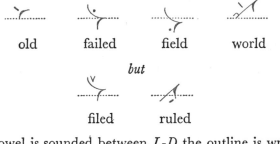

| old | failed | field | world |

but

| filed | ruled |

If a vowel is sounded between *L-D* the outline is written in full:

| followed | valued | married | relayed |

> **CHECK**
>
> **Scoop out curves F, V, L, R, SH, ZH.
> Make the shallow curves M, N, NG,
> MP, MB, flat and the right length**

SHORT FORMS

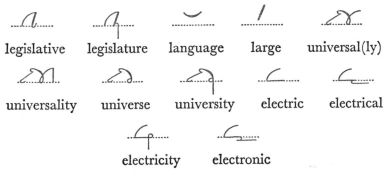

| legislative | legislature | language | large | universal(ly) |

| universality | universe | university | electric | electrical |

| electricity | electronic |

PHRASING
Downward *L* and Circle *S*:

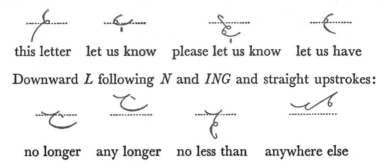

this letter   let us know   please let us know   let us have

Downward *L* following *N* and *ING* and straight upstrokes:

no longer   any longer   no less than   anywhere else

SHORT FORM AND PHRASING DRILL

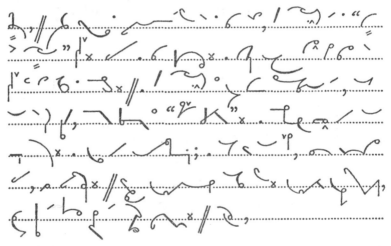

PREVIEW

eventually		finishing	
encounter		correspondence	
cushions		limitations	
allocated		geographical	

essential		numerical	
successful		extensively	
inexpert		rental	
inexperienced		cabinets	
downfall		purely	
conversant		consecutively	
alphabetical		index	
folder		combination	

Filing

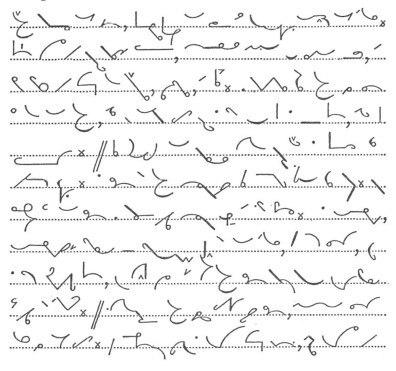

PREVIEW

legislature		convinced	
Parliament		puzzled	
citizens		actual	
protection		precisely	
deliberately		potential	
ignorance		alerted	
loyal		genuine	
avail		indicated	
befallen		absolutely	
discovered		fit	
allowance		explains	
quality		legal	

You and the Law

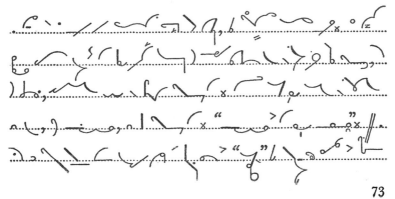

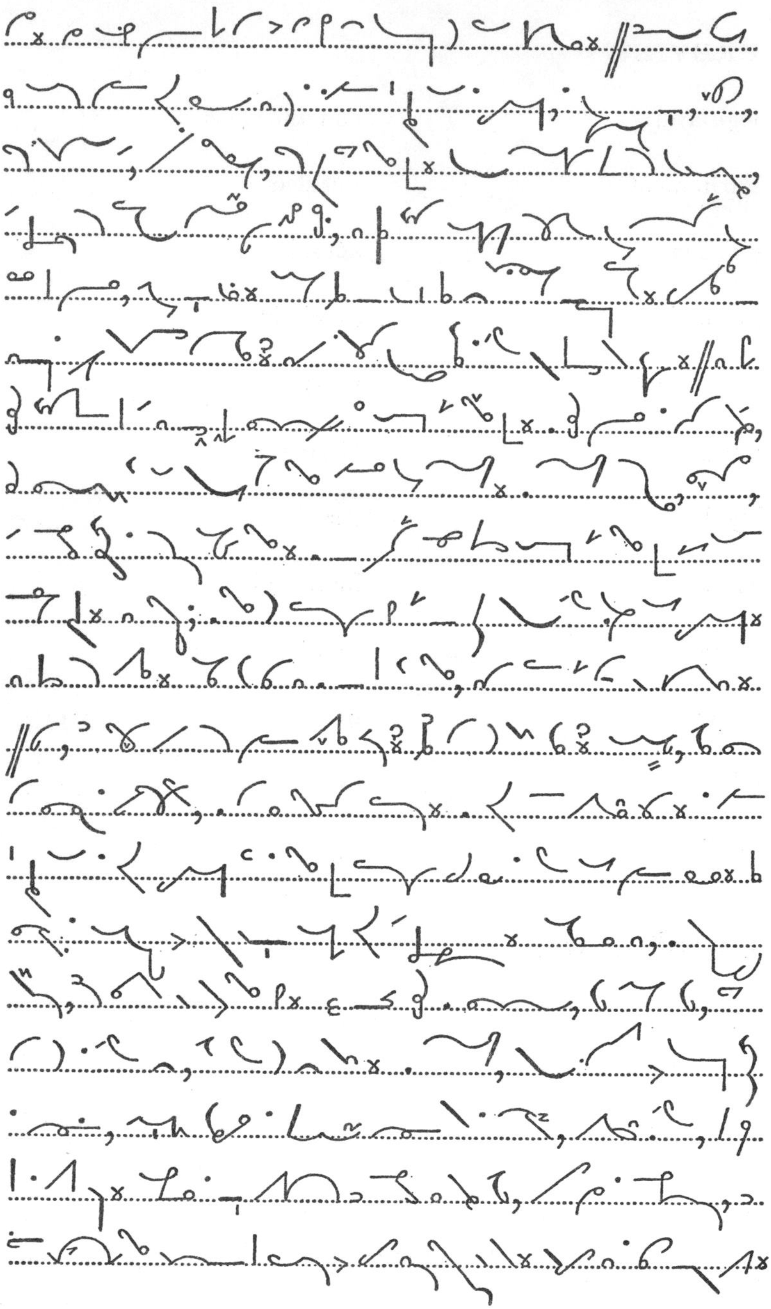

CORRESPONDENCE

Letter to:

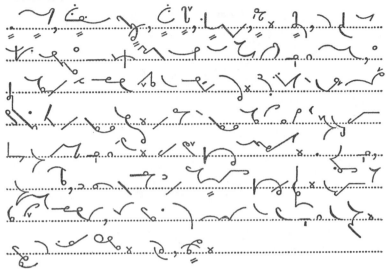

Letter to:

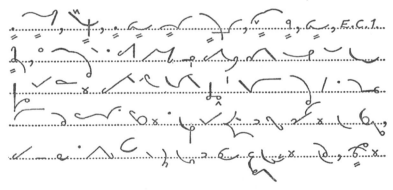

9 Hooks N and F/V

1 (a) A small hook at the end of a straight stroke on the side opposite to Circle *S* adds *N:*

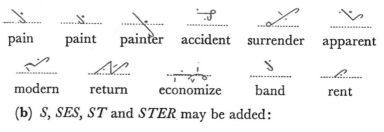

pain   paint   painter   accident   surrender   apparent

modern   return   economize   band   rent

(b) *S*, *SES*, *ST* and *STER* may be added:

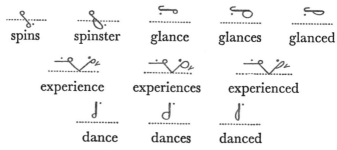

spins   spinster   glance   glances   glanced

experience   experiences   experienced

dance   dances   danced

2 (a) A small hook at the end of a curve adds *N*:

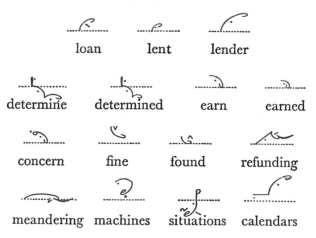

loan   lent   lender

determine   determined   earn   earned

concern   fine   found   refunding

meandering   machines   situations   calendars

(b) After a curve when a word ends with the light sound of *NS* (as in *fence*) the full stroke *N* is used with Circle *S*:

fence   announce   allowance

Compare

fens   nouns   lines

3 A small hook at the end of a straight stroke on the Circle *S* side adds *F* or *V*:

rave   raved   alternative   creative

private   profit   achieves   reserves

behaves   raves

4 Hooks for *N, F* and *V* are not used at the end of a word when a vowel follows the *N, F* or *V:*

pen	penny	men	many

fun	funny	cough	coffee

SHORT FORMS

been	general(ly)	within	southern	northern	behalf

advantage	difficult	can	cannot	deliverance

generalization	defective	deficient(ly)(cy)	difficulty

executive	expenditure	expense	financial(ly)	imperfect(ion)(ly)

perspective	demonstrate	English	Englishman	irrespective

irrespectively	January	executor

> **CHECK**
>
> **Make light strokes really light and heavy strokes will require only a slight increase in pressure**

PHRASING

Hook *N* may be used for:

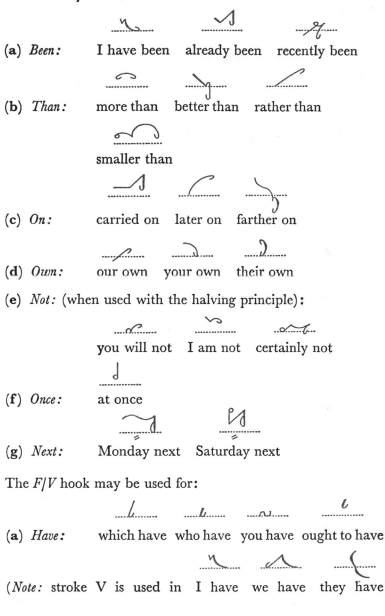

(a) *Been:*   I have been   already been   recently been

(b) *Than:*   more than   better than   rather than

               smaller than

(c) *On:*   carried on   later on   farther on

(d) *Own:*   our own   your own   their own

(e) *Not:* (when used with the halving principle):

               you will not   I am not   certainly not

(f) *Once:*   at once

(g) *Next:*   Monday next   Saturday next

The *F/V* hook may be used for:

(a) *Have:*   which have   who have   you have   ought to have

(*Note:* stroke V is used in   I have   we have   they have

79

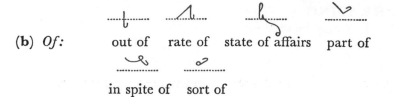

(b) *Of:*   out of   rate of   state of affairs   part of

in spite of   sort of

There are constant opportunities for using the Hook *F* to add *of*.

(c) *Off:*   set off   paid off

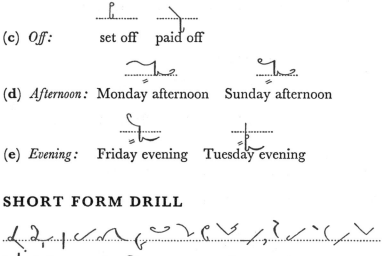

(d) *Afternoon:* Monday afternoon   Sunday afternoon

(e) *Evening:*   Friday evening   Tuesday evening

SHORT FORM DRILL

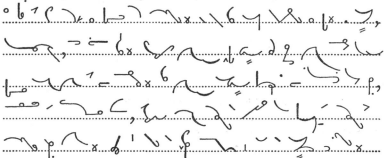

PHRASING DRILL

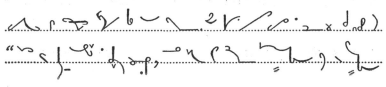

PREVIEW

beginning		shareholders
accounts		identical
quarterly		discernible
popularity		counsellor
petrol		attempted
convenient		precautions
transacting		deferred
discount		overdraft
facilities		currency
earners		irrespective
philanthropical		jewellery
campaigns		estate

Money and Banks

82

PREVIEW

feathers		adornment	
references		lethal	
dictates		ingredient	
artificial		ointment	
fascinating		wearer	
ancient		counteract	
adorned		overwhelming	
coloured		cleanliness	
European		standards	

powder	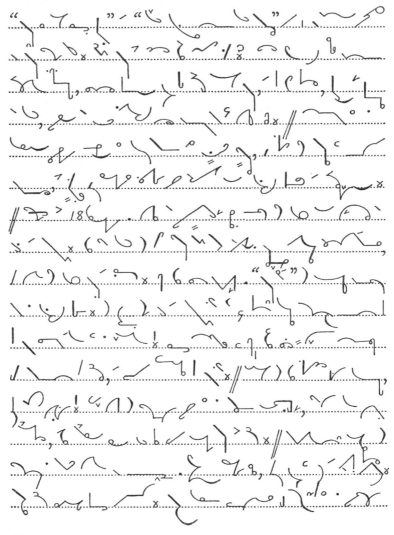	imported	
urgent		fragrant	
imperfections		partner	

Paint, Powder and Perfume

CORRESPONDENCE
This is a follow-up letter going out to many firms. A stencil would be cut.

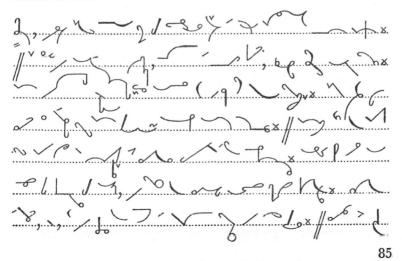

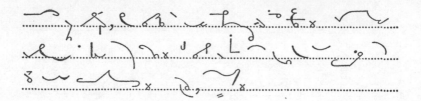

Memo to the Senior Filing Clerk:

10 Doubling

The doubling principle is the fastest principle in the Pitman system. Each doubled stroke represents at least three consonants. When doubling a stroke, make sure that you make it *at least* double the length of a regular stroke.

A good letter may lead to an interview.

Note that halved, doubled and regular length strokes are easily distinguished.

1 Curved strokes are doubled for the addition of -*TR*, -*DR*, -*THR* and, in a few common words -*TURE:*

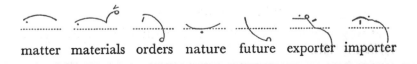

matter materials orders nature future exporter importer

87

2 Stroke *L* standing alone, or with Circle *S* added, is doubled only for -*TR:*

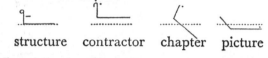

letters alters lighter later *but* ladder leader lather

3 Straight strokes are doubled for the addition of -*TR*, -*DR*, -*THR* and -*TURE:*

(**a**) When following another stroke:

structure contractor chapter picture

(**b**) When following Circle *S:*

scatter sector skater

(**c**) When there is a final joined diphthong:

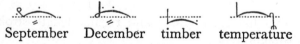

powder tutor pewter

(**d**) When there is a final hook:

tender render squander printer grafter

4 (**a**) *MP* and *MB* are doubled for the addition of *R*, giving a compound sound -*MPPR* or -*MBBR:*

September December timber temperature

(**b**) Another way to write -*MPPR* or -*MBBR* is to use the hook *R* to the compound consonant *MP*, *MB*, thus:

lumber camper hamper

This way is used when a more easily written and more legible outline results.

5 (a) *NG* is doubled for the addition of *KR* and *GR*, giving a compound consonantal sound *NGGR* or *NGKR:*

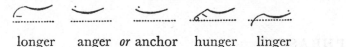

longer   anger *or* anchor   hunger   linger

(b) Similarly, another way to write -*NGKR*, -*NGGR* is to use the hook *R* to the consonant *NG*, thus:

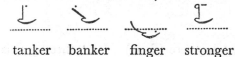

tanker   banker   finger   stronger

Again, this way is used when a more easily written and more legible outline results.

6 The doubling principle is not used:
(a) When there is a final vowel:

winter *but* wintry   secondary   boundary

(b) In the past tense:

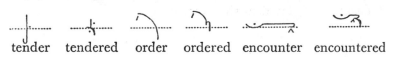

tender   tendered   order   ordered   encounter   encountered

---

> **CHECK**
>
> **Practise page turning. It should be a rapid and smooth action**

SHORT FORMS

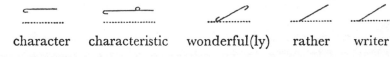

character   characteristic   wonderful(ly)   rather   writer

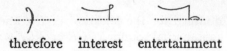

therefore   interest   entertainment

PHRASING

The **doubling** principle may be used in phrasing in the following ways:

1 *There/Their:* in there (their)   I am sure there is

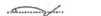

taking their   etc.

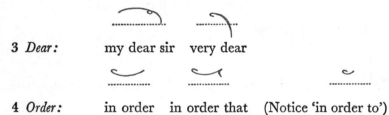

2 *Other:*   some other way in other words in other times

3 *Dear:*   my dear sir   very dear

4 *Order:*   in order   in order that   (Notice 'in order to')

SHORT FORM DRILL

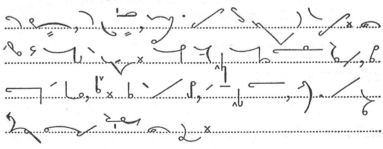

PHRASING DRILL

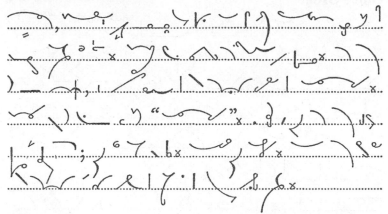

PREVIEW

amateur		executed	
disorder		signature	
clatter		operator	
watchful		anchor	
overseas		director	
feature		supervisor	
beholder		contribution	
character		programme	
flatter		interpret	
ambassadors		inquiries	
returned		congratulations	
folder		channelled	

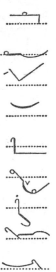

Office Order

PREVIEW

natural		wintry	
mother		factor	
father		inhabitants	
announces		yearn	
intention		freighter	
wander		borders	
encountered		bolder	
oyster		prospectors	
departure		malingerers	
adventure		masqueraders	
lighter		conjecture	
sombre		inflicting	

Work and Adventure

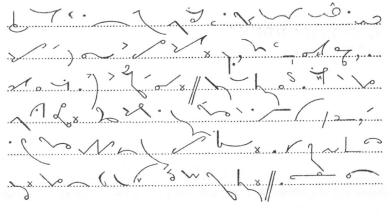

93

CORRESPONDENCE
A letter from:

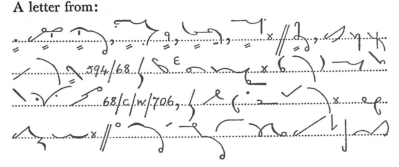

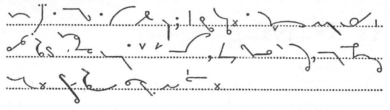

Memo to all members of the Sales Department, today's date,
from the Director.

11 Halving

1 In words of one syllable light strokes without a final hook or joined diphthong are halved for *T* only; heavy strokes for *D* only:

chat fat plate grade goods void deeds mat

2 In words of more than one syllable strokes may be halved for *T* or *D:*

debit indeed attached occurred arrived answered

noted reserved rapid

3 When a stroke has a final hook or a joined diphthong it may be halved for *T* or *D*, whether it is a word of one syllable or not:

96

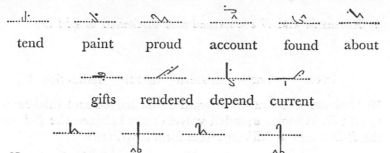

tend	paint	proud	account	found	about

gifts	rendered	depend	current

Note: doubt *but* doubts   drought *but* droughts

4 *RAY* is not halved unless joined to another stroke or unless it has a final hook:

write	written	rates	rents

5 *RT* at the end of a word is usually represented by half-length *RAY:*

report	export	start	support	part	smart

6 *-TED* and *-DED* at the end of a word are represented by a half-length *T* or *D:*

painted	bounded	coated	padded

7 Following stroke *T* or *D*, *-TED*, *-DED* are disjoined:

dictated	consolidated	credited	dated

8 Half-length *H*, when not joined to another stroke, is always written upwards:

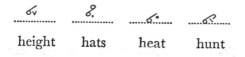

height	hats	heat	hunt

97

9 Strokes *M* and *N* are halved and thickened to add *D:*

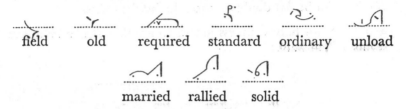

made aimed modern middle indication

10 Downward *L* and downward *R* are halved and thickened to add *D*. Where a sounded vowel comes between the *L-D* or the *R-D* then the full consonant form is written:

field old required standard ordinary unload

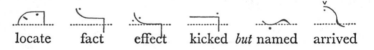

married rallied solid

11 The last stroke of an outline cannot be halved if there is a final vowel:

pit *but* pity need *but* needy

12 A stroke is not halved if the halving would not clearly show:

locate fact effect kicked *but* named arrived

SHORT FORMS

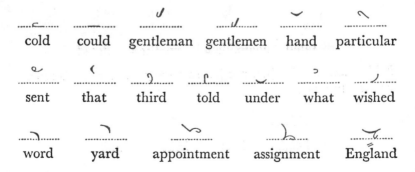

cold could gentleman gentlemen hand particular

sent that third told under what wished

word yard appointment assignment England

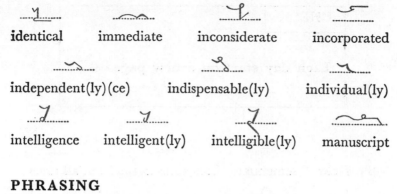

| identical | immediate | inconsiderate | incorporated |

independent(ly)(ce)   indispensable(ly)   individual(ly)

intelligence   intelligent(ly)   intelligible(ly)   manuscript

PHRASING
Use is made of the halving principle in phrasing as follows:

(a) *It:*   if it   I think it is   from it

(b) *To:*   able to   I am able to   unable to

I am unable to

(c) *Not:*   I am not   you will not   you are not

certainly not   they are not

(d) *Word:*   few words   in other words   to say a few words

(e) *Would:*   I would   this would   we would be

we would like

99

```
┌─────────┐
│ CHECK   │
└─────────┴──────────────────────┐
                                 │
  Each day start on a new page   │
                                 │
└────────────────────────────────┘
```

(f) *Time:*   some time   from time to time   at all times

at the same time

(g) *Part:*   in all parts   in all parts of the world

your part   for my part

SHORT FORM DRILL

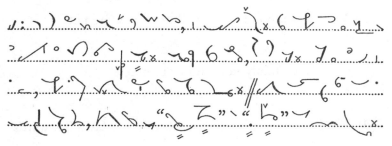

PHRASING DRILL

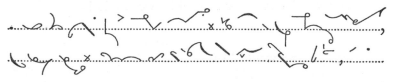

PREVIEW

duplicated		electronic*	
photographic		photographs	
transfer		restricted	
processes		hundreds	
incurred		fastest	
coloured		eventually	
standard		exhausted	
typewriter		replica	
claimed		disadvantages	
narrowed		vegetable	
original		urgency	
instant		economic	

* A shorter outline for an increasingly common word.

Duplicated Work

PREVIEW

described		pitfalls	
startling		indispensable	
abruptness		unhesitatingly	
achieved		assist	
diplomacy		somewhat	
nevertheless		finished	
valued		incorporated	
patience		tactful	
fortified		differentiate	
receptionist		intelligence	

telephonist ⟨shorthand⟩ hypocritical ⟨shorthand⟩

irate ⟨shorthand⟩ hurting ⟨shorthand⟩

Tact

⟨12 lines of Pitman shorthand outlines⟩

CORRESPONDENCE
Letter to:

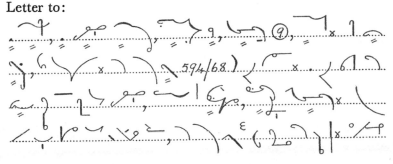

Type a draft of the following agenda:

12 Representation of H

1 The upward form of *H* (*HAY*) is generally used:

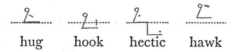

heavy   hurry   half   hundred   behind   adhere   hesitation

2 Downward *HAY* is used:

(**a**) When *H* is the only stroke in a word, and derivatives from such words:

high   highway   higher   highest   hay   haystack   he

(**b**) Before *K* and *G:*

hug   hook   hectic   hawk

Note: In outlines such as:

mahogany   coherence   unhook

where *H* is preceded by a horizontal stroke, downward *HAY* is used.

107

3 Tick *H* is used before *M*, upward *L* and downward *R:*

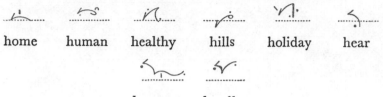

home	human	healthy	hills	holiday	hear

harmony	hardly

4 To obtain a shorter outline or avoid an awkward joining *H* may be represented in the middle of a word by a dot alongside the vowel sign:

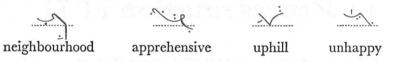

neighbourhood	apprehensive	uphill	unhappy

leasehold	perhaps

Note: In practice many outlines can be read without the dot and it may be omitted.

5 The prefix *IN-* before *HAY* is represented by a small hook except in the case of negative words, when the full stroke *N* is used:

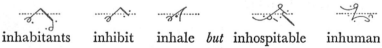

inhabitants	inhibit	inhale	*but* inhospitable	inhuman

SHORT FORMS

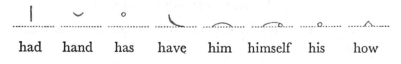

had	hand	has	have	him	himself	his	how

PHRASING

1 The word *he* is represented by the short form ⌐ in the middle or at the end of a phrase. In other cases ⌐ is used.

if he	if he would	when he	he	he will	he can

2 In a few phrases *HAY* may sometimes be omitted, or the form of an outline may be changed to do without it altogether:

I hope you will	we hope	in the house	to the house

SHORT FORM AND PHRASING DRILL

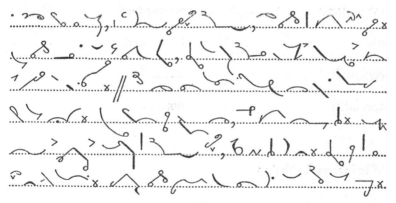

109

PREVIEW

unhappy		highlights	
unhealthy		interior	
nutritional		pavement	
harmony		continental	
habits		orchestras	
foreign		personalities	
restaurants		concentrate	
areas		daring	
inhabitants		guaranteed	
dishes		frightened	
regional		dissuade	
specialities		homely	

Wining and Dining

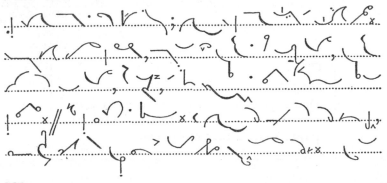

110

PREVIEW

deliberately		radiator	
hinder		lubrication	
handling		margin	
hook		appropriate	
session		query	
hidden		hesitation	
scattered		experts	
centring		dictation	
hump		hang	
enormous		hurrying	
hardly		dictator	
eraser		volume	

Habits (1)

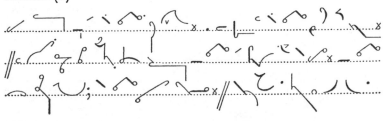

112

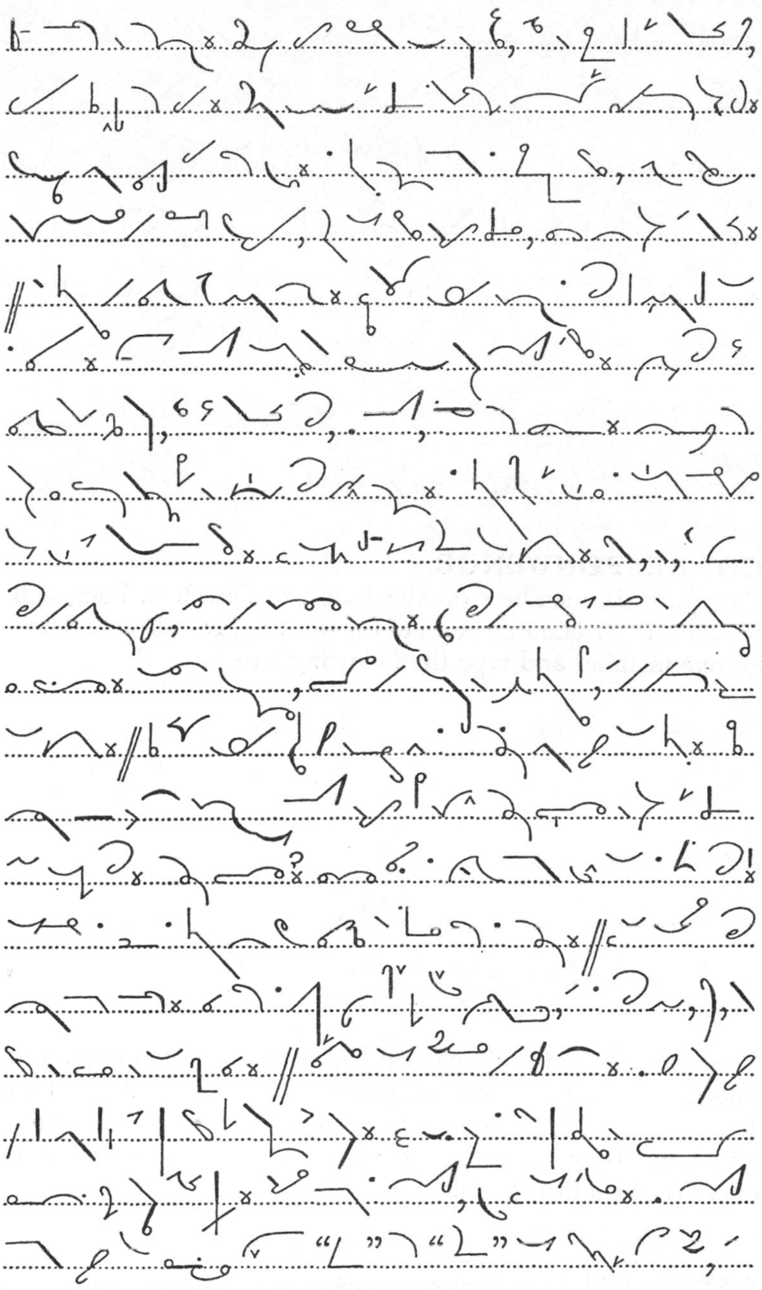

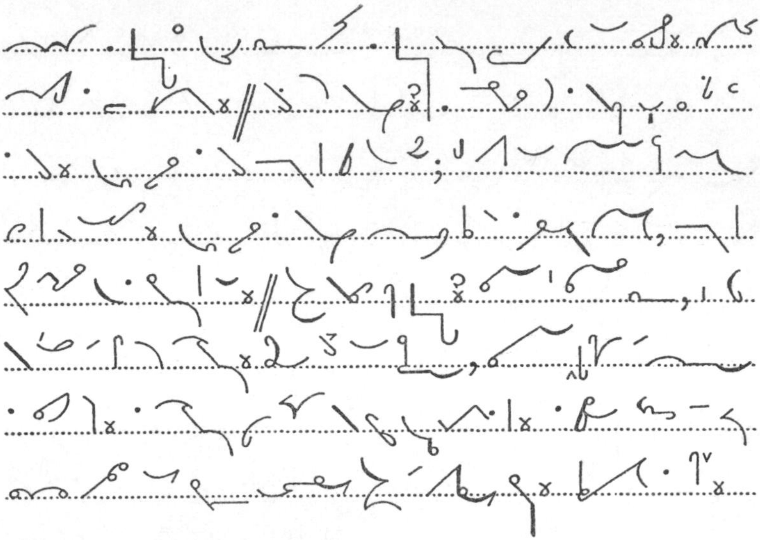

CORRESPONDENCE

There are six members on the Board of Directors. Each will receive a letter of notification of the meeting. Decide on a name for one member and type the following letter:

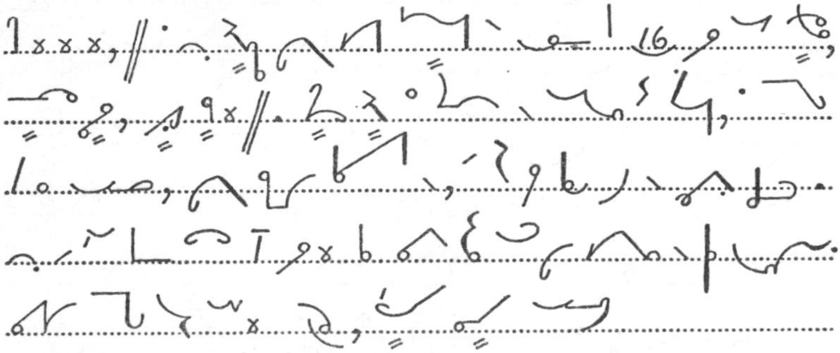

Please telephone the Barclaycard Centre at Northampton and inform them that I have misplaced my credit card but that I am treating this as lost or possibly stolen. Ask them to stop all payments on the present card and to issue me with a new one. Write confirming this.

929-123-456-789.x

13 Consonants S, Z and SH

1 The sound of *S* or *Z* is represented by a small circle written inside curves, outside angles, and with the left (counterclockwise) motion to straight strokes:

licence   system   source   risk   justice   succeeds

absorbs   serious   support   suburb   safely

2 The sound of *S* can be combined with *R* and *N* hooks to straight strokes by writing the *S*-circle on the hook side of the stroke:

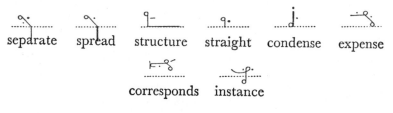

separate   spread   structure   straight   condense   expense

corresponds   instance

116

3 When combined with other hooks, the hook and Circle *S* are both shown:

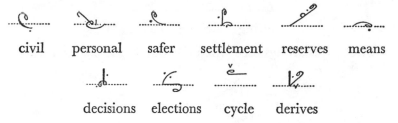

civil personal safer settlement reserves means

decisions elections cycle derives

4 When following another circle or loop the circle *S* is written thus, through the strokes:

successes suggests exercises administers

5 Stroke *S* is used at the beginning of an outline:
    (a) If a vowel comes before the *S*:

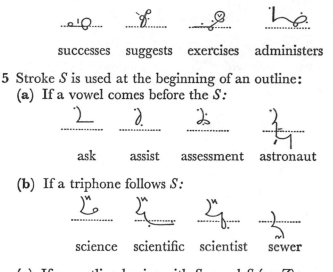

ask assist assessment astronaut

    (b) If a triphone follows *S*:

science scientific scientist sewer

    (c) If an outline begins with *S*-vowel-*S* (or *Z*):

size cease societies season Sussex

    (d) If *S* is the only consonant in the word:

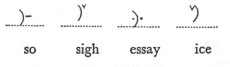

so sigh essay ice

or derivatives of these words:

sowing   sighing   icing

6 Stroke *Z* is always used when the sound of *Z* begins a word:

zeal   zero   zenith   zinc

7 Stroke *S* or *Z* is used at the end of an outline:
(**a**) If a vowel follows *S* or *Z*:

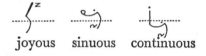

policy   busy   lazy   hazy

(**b**) If a word ends with a diphthong followed by *-OUS*:

joyous   sinuous   continuous

Note:

possess   access   precise   excess

8 Stroke *SH* is usually written downward:

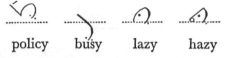

shake   shape   shattered

It is sometimes written upwards to obtain a better outline, and when it follows the direction of a curve:

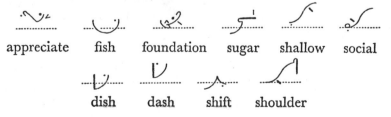

appreciate   fish   foundation   sugar   shallow   social

dish   dash   shift   shoulder

118

SHORT FORMS

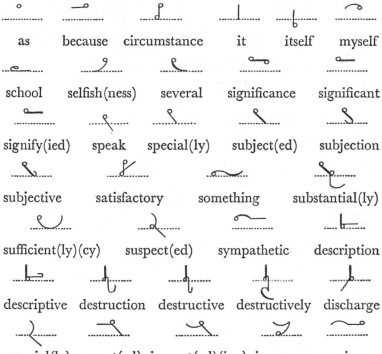

as	because	circumstance	it	itself	myself

school	selfish(ness)	several	significance	significant

signify(ied)	speak	special(ly)	subject(ed)	subjection

subjective	satisfactory	something	substantial(ly)

sufficient(ly)(cy)	suspect(ed)	sympathetic	description

descriptive	destruction	destructive	destructively	discharge

especial(ly)	expect(ed)	inspect(ed)(ion)	insurance	maximum

CHECK

After transcribing a page of notes put a pen or pencil stroke across the page to indicate it has been completed

---

PHRASING

In phrases the Circle *S* is used to represent:

1 *US:*

with us	tell us	help us	give us	against us

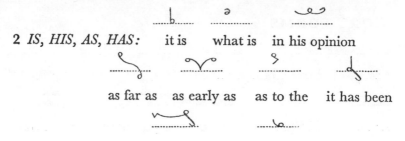

2 *IS, HIS, AS, HAS:*   it is   what is   in his opinion

as far as   as early as   as to the   it has been

I know there has been   if it is

Many other useful phrases involve the use of the Circle *S:*

yours truly   it seems   dear sirs   because it is   it is not

SHORT FORM DRILL

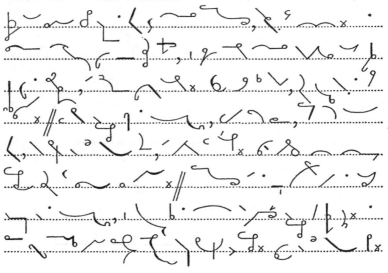

PHRASING DRILL

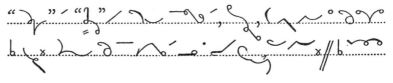

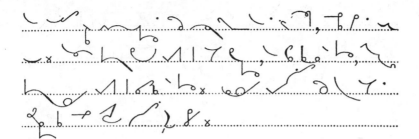

PREVIEW

spiral		access	
mistaken		possess	
fraction		dictionary	
flicked		transcription	
fingers		precious	
significant		continuous	
substantial		inefficiency	
filled		laziness	
sharpened		scientific	
sympathetic		vital	
hearing		discharge	
instrument		electronics	

Habits (2)

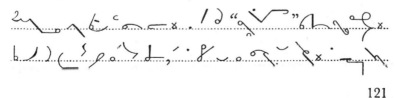

121

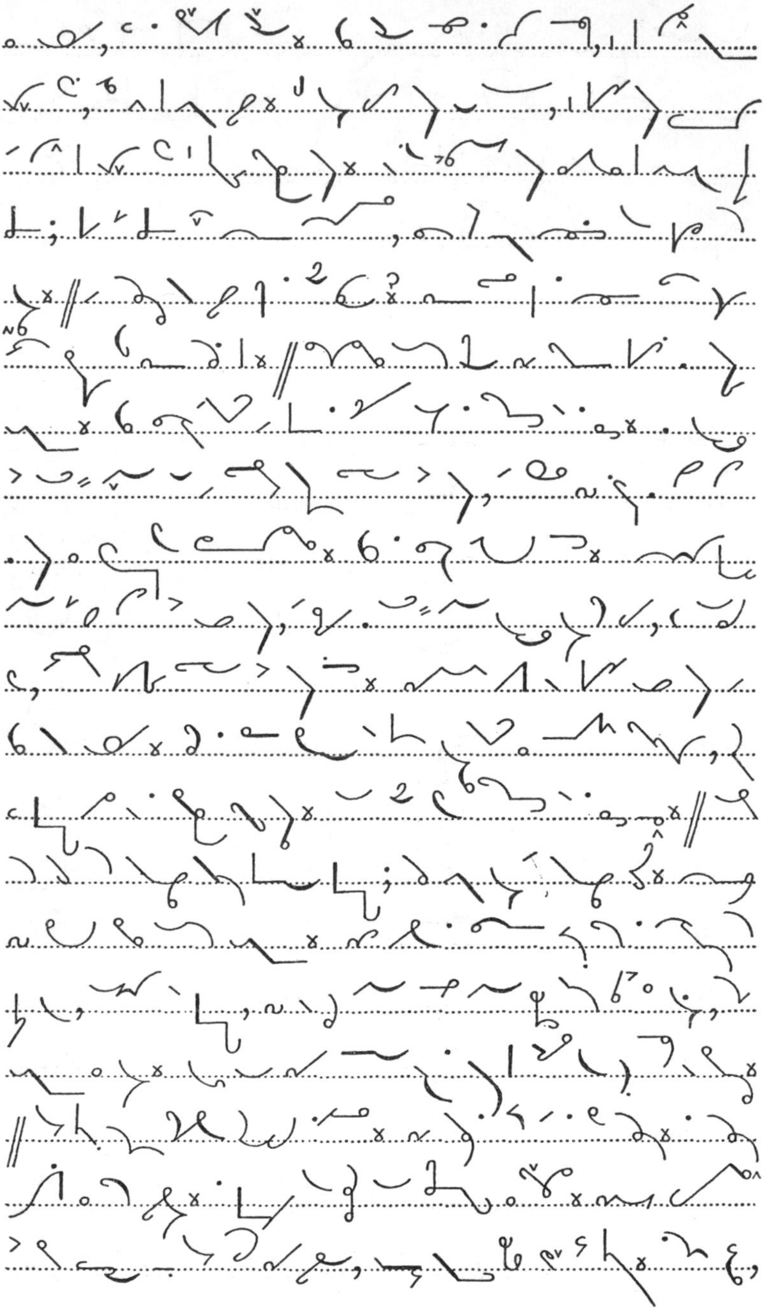

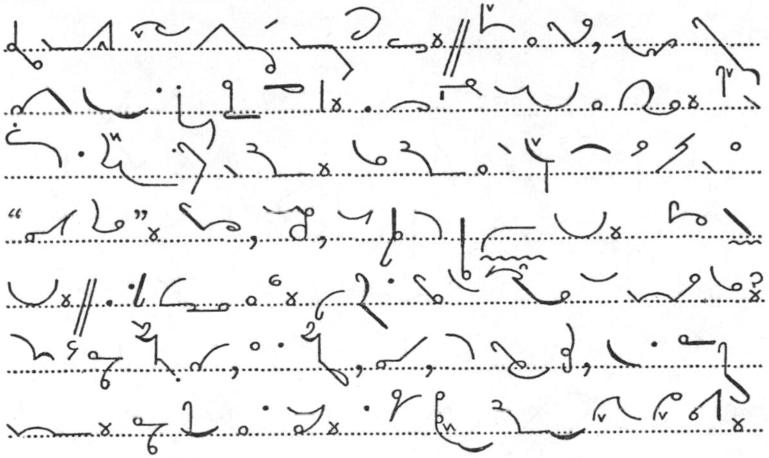

[shorthand outlines]

PREVIEW

consists	*[shorthand]*	deciphering	*[shorthand]*
preference	*[shorthand]*	personnel	*[shorthand]*
persistent	*[shorthand]*	compiled	*[shorthand]*
insistence	*[shorthand]*	issued	*[shorthand]*
persuasions	*[shorthand]*	compiler	*[shorthand]*
communications	*[shorthand]*	stencils	*[shorthand]*
salutation	*[shorthand]*	circular	*[shorthand]*
complimentary	*[shorthand]*	aside	*[shorthand]*
recipient	*[shorthand]*	similarly	*[shorthand]*
sender	*[shorthand]*	process	*[shorthand]*
reverse	*[shorthand]*	continuous	*[shorthand]*
safer	*[shorthand]*	zeal	*[shorthand]*

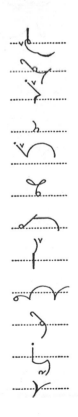

Office Correspondence

CORRESPONDENCE
A letter from:

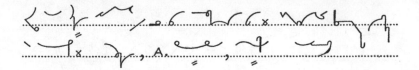

Memo:

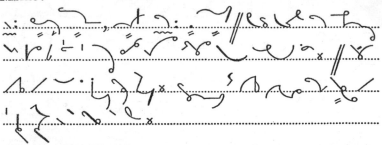

14 Loops ST and STR

1 The rules for writing the *ST* loop are similar to those for writing Circle *S*. The loop is written half the length of the stroke, and it should be written 'flat' and not 'fat':

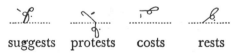					
staff	storage	story	sticker	stimulate	store

protest	amazed	arrest	experienced	artistic	statistic

2 Circle *S* can be added to the *ST* loop:

suggests	protests	costs	rests

3 The *ST* loop is not used:

(**a**) If there is a strongly sounded vowel between the *S* and *T:*

receipt	deceit	beset

(b) If a vowel follows *ST:*

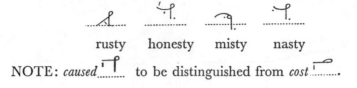

rusty honesty misty nasty

NOTE: *caused*  to be distinguished from *cost* .

4 The rules for writing the *STR* loop are similar to those for Circle *S*, but it is used only in the middle or at the end of a word. The loop is written two-thirds along the length of the stroke. It is written 'fat' to distinguish it clearly from the 'flat' *ST* loop,

e.g. fast and faster .

master masterpiece register administer investor

duster

5 Circle *S* can be added to the *STR* loop:

posters spinsters monsters barristers

6 The *STR* loop is not used:

(a) If there is a strongly sounded vowel between the *ST* and *R:*

restore moisture pasture

(b) If a vowel follows *STR:*

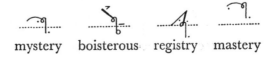

mystery boisterous registry mastery

128

SHORT FORMS

most	next	surprised	distinguish(ed)	investment	first

PHRASING

1 The *ST* loop makes some joining of words easier:

last year	last few years	just now

2 *First:* at first at first hand very first *Note:*— firstly

first of all for the first time

3 *Next:* Wednesday next Saturday next

CHECK

Use the notebook fully opened flat on the desk, and at right angles to the body

---

SHORT FORM AND PHRASING DRILL

PREVIEW

average		state	
specialized		province	
certificates		reporter	
executives		apprenticeship	
qualified		boisterous	
prepared		aroused	
privilege		participants	
advertisements		prisoner	
verbatim		barristers	
reporting		prosecutor	
conference		advisers	
arbitration		solicitors	

130

High Speed Writing (1)

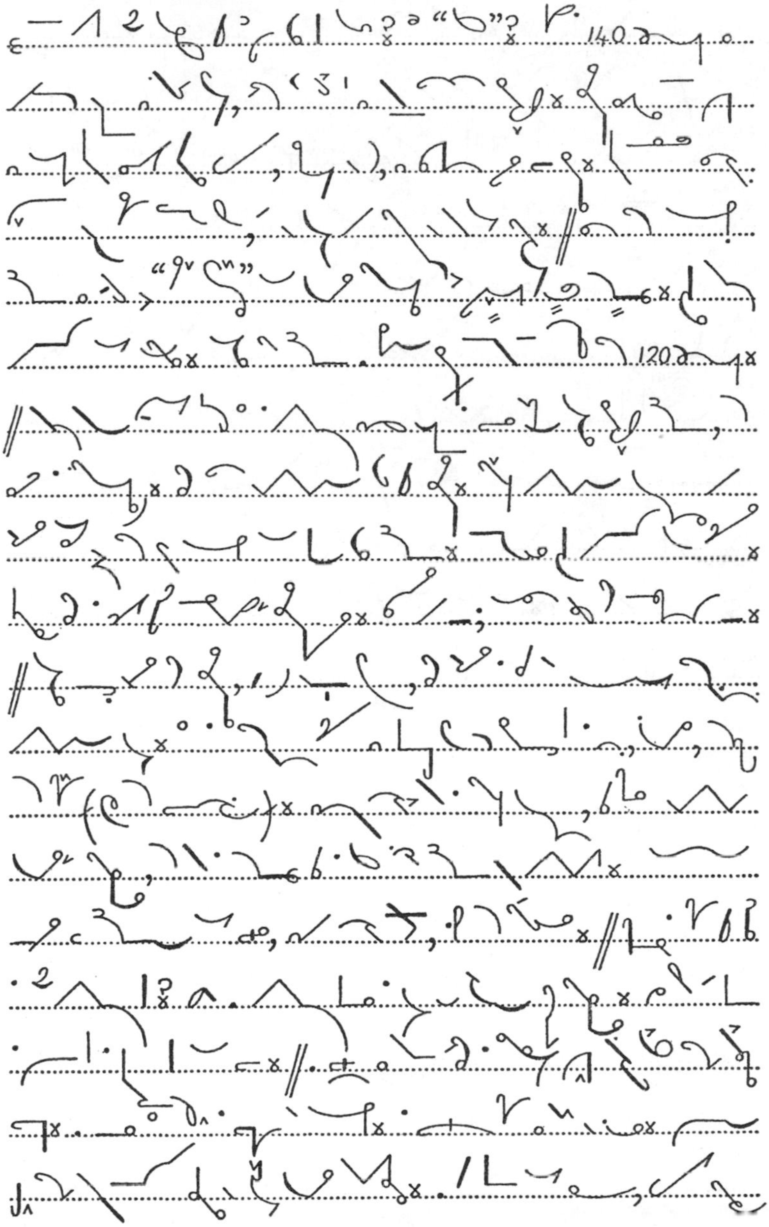

PREVIEW

completed		securely	
sorted		prevent	
operational		astray	
assigned		stamped	
indicated		notation	
envelopes		discrepancy	
sealed		appropriate	

132

unsealed	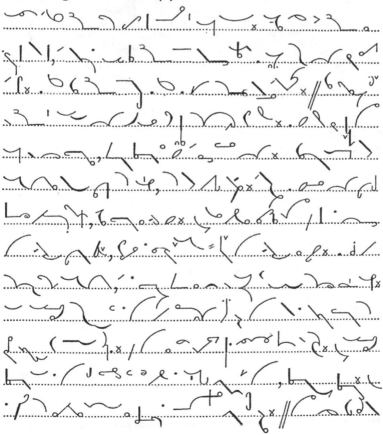	occasionally	
mechanical		alternatively	
opener		confidential	
justified		distributed	
enclosures		requests	

Handling Office Mail (1)

CORRESPONDENCE

Type the following notice for display on the Staff Notice
Board:

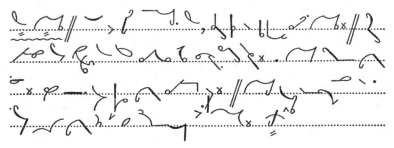

Letter to:

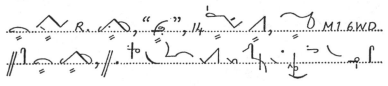

15 Circles Sway and Sez

1 The sound of *SW* at the beginning of a word is represented by a large circle. The *SW* circle is written in the same direction as the Circle *S :*

swinging   swift   swim   swear   switch   sweeter   sweeper

2 The *SW* circle is used only at the beginning of an outline.

persuade   persuasion   glassware   sway

3 The sound *SES, SEZ* in the middle or at the end of a word is represented by a large circle. A vowel other than short 'e' vowel coming between the two *S*'s is written inside the large circle.

necessary   possessive   houses   success   ceases   successes

136

exercises   emphasizes   exhaust   decisive

4 *SEZ* can be combined with the *N* hook:

references   chances   experiences   assurances

SHORT FORMS

all	any	aught	be	beyond	but

different(ce)	do	for	go	important(ce)	me

much	of	on	owe	put	shall	short

thank(ed)	them	themselves	thing	think	though

thus	to be	usual	to	was	when	who

whose	why	without	you	young	yesterday

unanimous(ly)	minimum	never	nevertheless	nothing

notwithstanding   ourselves

PHRASING
The *SW* circle is used for:

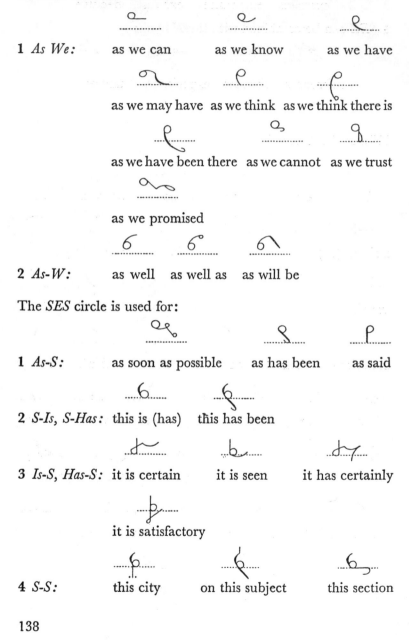

1 *As We:*   as we can   as we know   as we have

as we may have as we think as we think there is

as we have been there as we cannot as we trust

as we promised

2 *As-W:*   as well   as well as   as will be

The *SES* circle is used for:

1 *As-S:*   as soon as possible   as has been   as said

2 *S-Is, S-Has:* this is (has)   this has been

3 *Is-S, Has-S:* it is certain   it is seen   it has certainly

it is satisfactory

4 *S-S:*   this city   on this subject   this section

138

5 The *SEZ* circle standing alone:

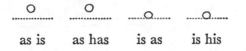

| as is | as has | is as | is his |

SHORT FORM DRILL

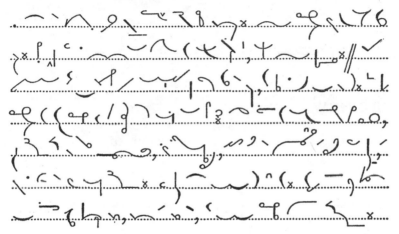

```
CHECK

Phrase whenever possible and make
full use of short forms
```

PHRASING DRILL

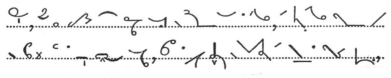

PREVIEW

silence		unannounced	
ceases		occurrences	
traditional		conclusion	
distinguished		pathologist	
prisoner		deceased	
escorted		sworn	
officers		declaration	
indictment		cross-examination	
adjourned		accuracy	
outlining		interrupt	
witnesses		straightforward	
appearances		unfolding	

140

High Speed Writing (2)

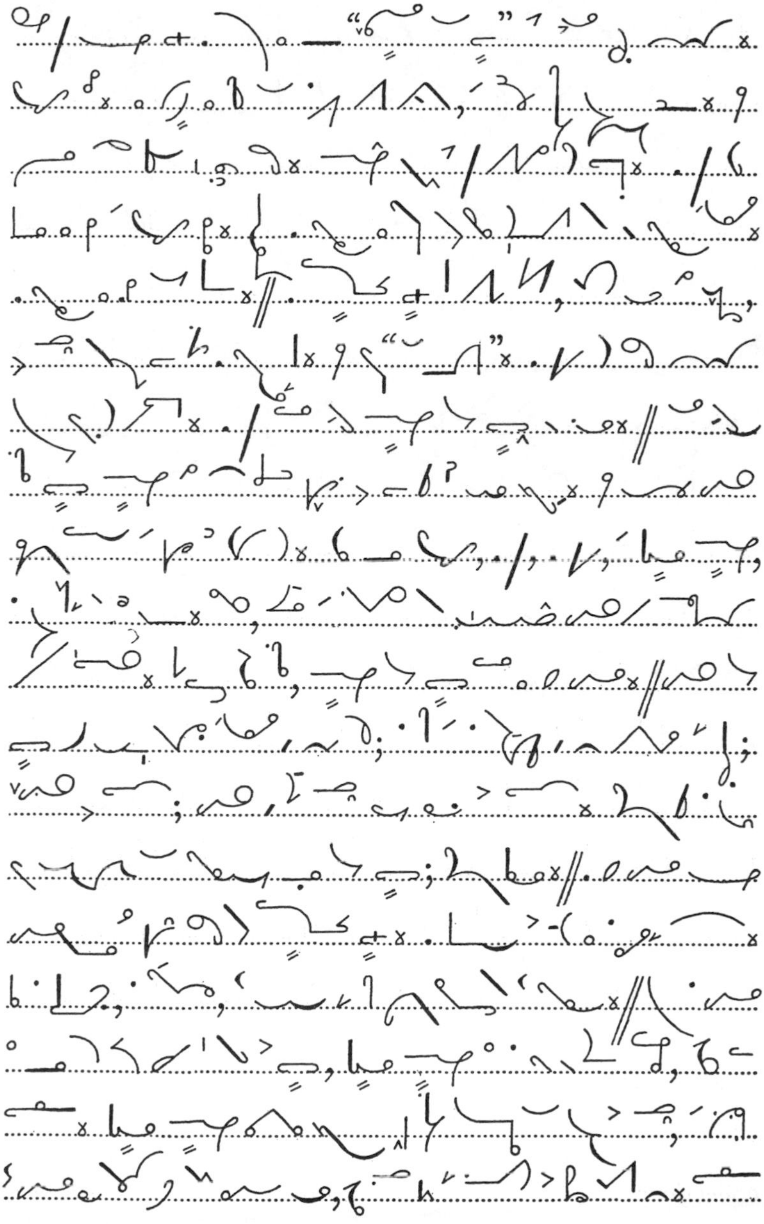

PREVIEW

wisest .... separated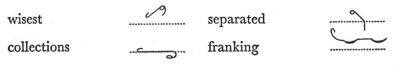

collections .... franking

142

process		adjusted		
enclosures		postal		
mentioned		emphasized		
registered		co-operation		
excessive		criticisms		
postage		indistinct		
leaflets		unintelligible		
current		swamp		
prefers		sooner		
sizes		efficiently		

Handling Office Mail (2)

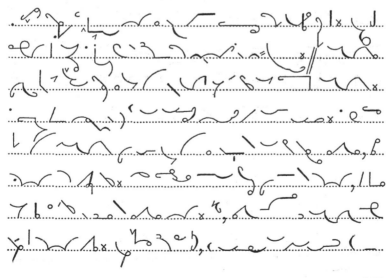

CORRESPONDENCE
A circular letter to all customers:

Using the firm's address as a heading, type out an advertisement for the national papers giving the information used in the circular letter.